FALL DOWN 7 TIMES GET UP 8

Praise for *Fall Down 7 Times, Get Up 8*

"A truly fresh take on getting more from our kids! Read this book if you want to work smarter instead of harder and to bring enthusiasm back to your classroom or school."

Scott Bailey, Principal
Waskom Middle School, TX

"This is a 'must read' book for anyone desiring to help young people become confident, self-directed learners. Readers will walk away not only challenged in their thinking but with a multitude of strategies that help students develop the internal motivation so necessary for success in today's world."

Patti Kinney, Associate Director
NASSP, Reston, VA

"The joy and energy that Debbie Silver brings to her amazing presentations shine on each page of this book. Every teacher will appreciate Silver's enthusiasm and positive outlook. Use this book to infect your students with a love for learning!"

Dr. Danny Brassell, Author, Speaker,
and Founder lazyreaders.com

"Debbie Silver's insightful book is a must-read for anyone ready to embrace proven skills to help kids motivate themselves for success. Discarding practices that don't work, she illustrates parenting and classroom strategies that teach children productive habits, happiness, and inspiration. This book will be shared and recommended for years to come!"

Dr. Monte Selby, Educational Speaker,
Author, and Songwriter

"Dr. Silver brings together the key aspects of motivating young learners that help teachers and parents develop self-directed individuals. She presents important frameworks in accessible ways along with actionable, proven techniques. Recommended reading!"

Eduardo Briceño, CEO
Mindset Works

DEBBIE SILVER

FALL DOWN 7 TIMES GET UP 8

TEACHING KIDS TO SUCCEED

FOREWORD BY CAROL ANN TOMLINSON

A Joint Publication

CORWIN
A SAGE Company

AMLE™

CORWIN

A SAGE Company

FOR INFORMATION

Corwin
A SAGE Company
2455 Teller Road
Thousand Oaks, California 91320
(800) 233-9936
www.corwin.com

SAGE Publications Ltd.
1 Oliver's Yard
55 City Road
London, EC1Y 1SP
United Kingdom

SAGE Publications India Pvt. Ltd.
B 1/I 1 Mohan Cooperative Industrial Area
Mathura Road, New Delhi
India 110 044

SAGE Publications Asia-Pacific Pte. Ltd.
3 Church Street
#10-04 Samsung Hub
Singapore 049483

Acquisitions Editor: Arnis Burvikovs
Associate Editor: Desirée A. Bartlett
Editorial Assistant: Kimberly Greenberg
Production Editor: Cassandra Margaret
Seibel
Copy Editor: Codi Bowman
Typesetter: Hurix Systems Pvt. Ltd
Proofreader: Wendy Jo Dymond
Indexer: Terri Corry
Cover Illustration and Design: Peter H.
Reynolds
Permissions Editor: Karen Ehrmann

Printed in the United States of America.

Library of Congress Cataloging-in-Publication Data

Silver, Debbie, 1950–
Fall down 7 times, get up 8 : teaching kids to succeed / Debbie Silver.

p. cm.

Includes bibliographical references and index.

ISBN 978-1-4129-9877-2 (pbk.)

1. Motivation in education. I. Title. II. Title:
Fall down seven times, get up eight.

LB1065.S544 2012

370.15′4—dc23

2012001337

This book is printed on acid-free paper.

15 16 17 10 9 8 7 6 5

Contents

3. Self-Regulation, Deliberate Practice, and Failure 35

*That's what learning is, after all; not whether we lose the
game, but how we lose and how we've changed because of
it and what we take away from it that we never had before,
to apply to other games. Losing, in a curious way, is
winning.—Richard Bach*

4. Attribution Theory—Why Did I Succeed (or not)? 55

*Whether you think you can, or you think you can't,
you're probably right.—Henry Ford*

5. Mindset—The Key to Self-Motivation 75

*You have a choice. Mindsets are just beliefs. They're
powerful beliefs, but they're just something in your
mind, and you can change your mind.—Carol Dweck*

Quality is never an accident; it is the result of high intention, sincere effort, intelligent direction and skillful execution; it represents the wise choice of many alternatives.—attributed to Willa Foster

Foreword

Joan White became one of my private heroes as I had the opportunity to observe and teach her five children during my years as a public school teacher. In the beginning, I knew her just as a pleasant parent who, like most parents, wanted her children to fare well in school. In the beginning, I knew her kids as ones who giggled more than most. It took longer for me to realize that the five teenagers inevitably but subtly stood out a bit from their peer groups in ways that suggested thoughtful parenting.

It wasn't that they were perfect kids. There's no such thing. It wasn't that they avoided the typical adolescent miscalculations in decision making. That's part of growing up. What set them apart seemed to be a maturity of perspective—a sort of grounding—that I thought at the time was a kind of emergent wisdom.

I knew the Whites to be a middle-class family by virtue of neighborhood. The kids dressed more or less like their classmates. I did notice, after a while, however, that although the kids' clothes were standard issue early adolescent style, none of the kids had many outfits—maybe one or two more than the days of the week would require. I didn't think much of it. I was impressed that with five kids, their clothes were always clean and unwrinkled.

The small moments that added up to my sense that these kids were firmly grounded were many and unfolded slowly.

I recall a time when one of the boys badly wanted to attend an evening school event. I knew from overheard conversations that it mattered a lot to him to share the experience with his friends. Shortly before the date of the event, I heard him explain to a group of buddies that he wouldn't be there. I could see disappointment in his eyes, but with steadfastness not typical of the age group, he simply said, "It's my brother's birthday, and in my house, we celebrate birthdays together. No exceptions." No whining, blaming, bemoaning.

Then there was a time when I had just come home from a few days in the hospital following surgery. It was June, oppressively hot, and my house was full of unpacked boxes from a very recent, poorly timed, move. One of the White's boys had a friend staying with him for a few days. Joan woke the boys early on the summer morning, explaining that she wanted to let them know their options for the day early enough so they could make a good choice. They could, she explained, work with Mr. White to cut hay in the area behind their house, or they could go to Mrs. Tomlinson's house to help with some painting that needed to be done before the boxes from her move were unpacked. I was both surprised and exuberant to respond to the doorbell and find Ken and Bobby, paint brushes in hand, standing on the porch. They didn't seem resentful. They laughed a lot as they painted and did a better job than most professionals would. They came back for three days, voluntarily—no mother-imposed "choices"—just doing a job that needed doing. Just helping and making a good time of it in the process.

In our English class, the students had a lengthy and demanding final project that capped the eighth grade. This was in precomputer times, and many students brought in papers typed by parents who wanted the work to look good. Joan, too, typed the oldest child's paper, but with a caveat. That student would have to learn to type so he or she could type the second child's paper the following year—and so on down the line. Each year that followed, with good-natured grumbling, the next child in line started early to learn to type so the brother or sister who came next would have a competent typist for the project ahead.

Then there was the day of the sit-in at school. It was a time when protests of various sorts were common events in cities and on college campuses across the country. Some social leaders at school were angry because a popular student had been suspended for tardiness—the fourth step in what appeared to me to be a generous school tardy policy. Taking a lead from the news, they decided to hold a sit-in after second period. The school principal, who was a wise soul, got wind of the impending protest and decided that a confrontation was in no one's interest. So she came on the public address system as second period was about to end. She explained to the students that she understood they were unhappy with the tardy policy and wanted to express their feelings, and she gave students who were interested in making a statement permission to hold a five-minute sit-in. She explained exactly how things needed to work, and the students followed her directions precisely. It was a brilliant move.

Peter, the one of the White clan most likely to push the boundaries, was one of the protesters. At the end of the day, his mom arrived in the school parking lot to be one of the drivers for an overnight field trip for our English class. Still feeling heady from the power of the protest, Peter began to explain enthusiastically to Joan what had occurred earlier in the day.

As he began about the fourth or fifth sentence, she stopped him. "Let me be sure I understand what you're telling me," she said. "Are you saying that you were part of a group that decided to sit down in the hall to make a statement against school policy when you should have been in class?"

Still excited, Peter responded with a lilt, "Yes ma'am."

"Before you made that choice, did you take the time to understand how that policy came to be, Peter? Did you do anything to get the facts before you acted?"

Peter was a bit subdued, but still convinced of the rightness of his involvement. "No ma'am," he said. "I didn't do that, but it was okay because the principal gave us permission to have the sit-in."

"And did you consider that you were acting in defiance of a school leader who does so much to make this a great school," his mom continued. "Did it occur to you that things could have gotten out of hand? Would you have had the necessary insight to handle the situation if something had gone wrong?"

Now Peter looked stricken. He wasn't angry with his mother for taking the wind out of his sails. He was observably disappointed in himself. "Do you think it would be okay for me to take a few minutes and go inside to apologize before we leave for the trip?" he asked Joan without prompting.

Inside, he choked back tears and said to the principal, in part, "I let myself down today. I disappointed my mother. And I'm sure you must have felt disappointed in me too. When I made the decision to take part in the protest, I wasn't wise enough to realize the choice could have led to a situation I am not experienced enough to handle. And it didn't occur to me that my decision was disrespectful of your work. I want you to know I have learned something from this and will do my best to be a better citizen of the school as a result."

Not exactly a typical adolescent response.

Joan lived out the values Debbie Silver commends in this book. All of the kids were smart, but I never saw an indication that they felt they had more to contribute than any of their peers. They never felt entitled—at least not for long. They worked hard, not to make the best grades in the class, but always to do *their* best. If a job was hard to do, they learned to work harder. If they fell down seven times, they got up eight, sometimes with coaching from their parents. From that, they *earned* a sense of resilience and self-efficacy. There were always clear "fences" in their lives—boundaries they knew not to cross—but within those structures, they were guided in making thoughtful choices. They came to understand the centrality of family, loyalty to friends, gratitude to the many people who contributed to their betterment, and the compassion to reach out to people who need a hand.

I learned after knowing the family for many years, there was an additional "challenge" in raising the kids as Joan and her husband did. The family had access to considerable inherited wealth. That may not sound like much of a handicap, but abundance too often becomes a reason to feel entitled, to act from a sense of power and privilege, to overlook the contributions of people who are less well off. I've always found it interesting that this set of parents opted not to let their children know their futures were financially secure. They lived simply. They taught the kids to work for what they got and to appreciate what they had.

Over the years, I came to know the Whites well. The five kids now have teenagers of their own, and they stay in touch from time to time. Without exception, they are happy, productive, anchored adults who are passing on to their children the inner compass their parents helped them develop.

I think Joan would have liked this book. I think her children and their children would as well.

Carol Ann Tomlinson

Preface

Background

An ancient Japanese proverb states "Fall down seven times, get up eight." In March, 2011, northern Japan was hit by a magnitude 9 earthquake, the largest in their recorded history. Parts of Japan were literally destroyed. Hundreds of thousands were killed or maimed. With limited resources and scarcity of basic supplies, the Japanese people immediately stood together and began to rebuild. They were true to their proverb. This kind of demonstrated resilience is something desirable for all people. Adults want it for our children. But could we expect our country's younger generation to roll up their sleeves and face adversity with such tenacity? Or could we expect our children to demand that somebody else come and fix things for them?

Purpose

I can think of few life lessons as important to success as the beautiful metaphor "Fall down seven times, get up eight." Teachers and parents who want students to learn to be resilient, joyful, enduring learners must find a way to inspire self-motivation in students that will empower them to deal with whatever they encounter in life. Rather than trying to shield them from adversity and challenge, it is the job of adult advocates to push learners to the far reaches of their abilities and equip them with the tools they need to pursue goals through even the most difficult circumstances.

When giving presentations, I speak about the consensus of various cognitive and behavioral theorists who believe much of what adults do is counterproductive to the outcomes we really want for our children. We have given trophies to players who just show up, and we told our children they are *the best* when they clearly are not. We have led them to believe they have a right to be comfortable, to be untroubled, and to be constantly entertained. In an effort to ensure they feel good about themselves, we applaud, we excuse, we rationalize, and, when needed, we intervene on their behalf. And I ask this question, "How has that worked out so far?"

To audiences I explain my evolution from being a teacher who used abundant rewards, incentives, and praise to someone who has had to reconsider many of the well-meaning things I said and did to children, both my hundreds of students and my own children (three sons and two stepsons).

Invariably, at the end of presentations, audience members will seek me out to ask specifically about things they are doing with their students and/or offspring.

"Seriously, our child really is extremely bright. We all tell her how smart she is all the time because we want her to live up to her full potential. How can that be the wrong thing to do?"

"We told my son that if he will stick with his hockey lessons, we will let him get a new Xbox game. Was that bad?"

"In our district there is a big emphasis on differentiated instruction. I like what you are saying about the zone of proximal development, attribution theory, and mindsets. My goal is to give all my students an equal education. So which way is best?"

"Are you telling us that basically anyone can be anything they want if they just try hard enough? Is that what I tell my son?"

"We were told that our daughter's IQ is just below normal. We're not sure what that means, and we are worried that she won't be able to keep up in school. How do we keep her from giving up when she's up against such overwhelming odds?"

"At our school, we use a schoolwide reward system to encourage kids to read. I've never been comfortable with it, but most of the other teachers think it's a great idea. What do the experts say about that?"

"I teach high school. I have a student who is convinced that he cannot do the work in my class. He won't even try. He totally withdraws when I try to encourage him. I know for a fact he could do it, if he wanted to. Do you think he's just faking incompetence for some reason, or is there a possibility he really doesn't know how capable he is?"

"I've told my students that failure is not an option. I won't accept failures in my class. What's wrong with that?"

(My answers are in Chapter 10.)

Rationale

It finally occurred to me that what most parents and educators long for is a guide with specific strategies about how to help children become independent, successful learners. We need to understand the rationale of theory, but we also seek direction on how to foster autonomous, persistent visionaries rather than dependent, helpless victims. We want concrete examples about how to best change a generation of children who think they are entitled to a better life into a generation of children who are better able to make that life happen for themselves.

Most of the teachers and parents I know have a basic knowledge of motivational theory either from their experience or from their academic pursuits. There is a wealth of material written on the subject. The purpose of *Fall Down 7 Times, Get Up 8* is to synthesize the thinking of major motivational theorists into a framework of what to say and what not to say to children and why. My intent is to provide specific, applicable solutions to common encounters of adults who work with kids.

The suggested strategies are not always easy (some go against what we've been doing for years), but they are feasible and get easier with practice. We adults must act as meaningful role models who regularly articulate and demonstrate the value of personal responsibility, dedication, persistence, and resilience. We must be encouraging but honest with our charges; we must give them effective feedback that avoids labels (both positive and negative). We must judge less and guide more.

We have to teach our children they have power over their lives, and through their efforts and their choices, they can affect change in their circumstances and in their destinies. We can no longer perpetuate the myth "You can be anything in the world you want to be," but we must constantly remind them that through purposeful practice they can get better at anything they choose. We have to show them every day that effort and choices are things they can control, and in fact, they are the keys to a successful life.

Invitation to the Reader

I have worked in the field of education for more than 40 years. I am a teacher, a parent, a stepparent, a professor, an educational consultant, an author, and a grandmother. I work throughout this country and abroad on many issues dealing with motivation for both adults and children. I think the keys to successful schooling are inherently connected to how well we prepare our students to become self-sufficient, resourceful lifelong learners.

The concepts I present are not original; I have learned from experts in the fields of behavioral and cognitive psychology, from thoughtful theorists, and from countless teachers and students along the way. My ideas are not always politically correct.

They do not excuse any ethnicity, socioeconomic group, faith, culture, community, or family from being unable to empower its offspring. At this point I am not concerned as much with "why we are this way or that way" as I am about how we can make things better for every learner. This is a handbook for adult advocates who want to help kids become self-motivated lifelong learners rather than dependent short-term thinkers who think the world owes them a free ride.

I want to assure you that I did not initially embrace some of the concepts I present in this book, nor did I accept all of them with equal ease. These are the best practices I know *for now*. Some ideas may seem counterintuitive and others appear to be downright blasphemous to our educational system as it is now. But I know that even small steps can make a big difference in the ways we encourage children. I am continuing my growth as an advocate for children, and I invite you to join this journey as you see fit.

Acknowledgments

First I want to thank my sons for allowing me to tell their stories all these years to illustrate points I make in my speaking and my writing. I hope my daughters-in-law and grandchildren realize they are in for the same shameless exploitation, but theirs are the stories I know best.

I want to acknowledge Dr. Jeff Walzcyk at Louisiana Tech University who first piqued my interest in cognitive psychology and made me aware of attribution theory. Jeff, thank you for sharing your passion for learning and research with me.

And this book may have never been finished had it not been for the perseverance and encouragement of my editor, Arnis Burvikovs. Arnis, I appreciate you for keeping me focused and moving forward. Thanks, too, to Desirée Barlett, Kimberly Greenberg, Cassandra Seibel, Codi Bowman, and all of the phenomenal staff at Corwin. All of you have made this project a rewarding growth experience.

It is hard to find words to express the gratitude I have for Peter Reynolds and all the folks at FableVision who created the cover for this book. Pete, you are a constant source of inspiration to me as well as to educators around the world, and I am so thankful to share with you a vision of fulfillment for kids everywhere. And I offer a special note of appreciation to my former student, Ben Daily, who used his professional photography expertise to make my author photo look better than I do in real life.

I am honored that Dr. Carol Ann Tomlinson agreed to write the forward for my book. When I finished my manuscript and asked for feedback, Carol Ann was the first reviewer to offer encouragement, positive feedback, and constructive advice. Carol Ann, you are not only an expert in your field you are a true teacher in every sense of the word.

There is no way I would have had time to write this book while maintaining a speaking schedule if I did not have the world's greatest assistant, Dedra Stafford. Dedra, thank you for always being there and for making me look far more efficient than I am. You are a true associate and friend.

I must give credit for the inspiration of this manuscript to my best friend and husband, Dr. Lawrence Silver. Lawrence first introduced me to the work of Dr. Carol Dweck when he wrote his dissertation about motivation and the sales force in 2000. Lawrence, your unconditional support and faith in me are one of my greatest sources of motivation.

Finally, I want to give my heartfelt appreciation to the hundreds of teachers who have shared their narratives with me that have helped me clarify my thinking and have given me real-life examples to help me deepen my understanding of our profession and our challenge. Thank you for all of your insights and suggestions for this book. I truly appreciate those of you who helped me as I struggled to find a title. Ironically, I stumbled across the final choice while thumbing through a catalog and found the proverb printed on a decorative wall hanging. The minute I read it, I knew it was perfect for what we have been discussing about student motivation. Thank you for what you do every day for students and for being able to fall down seven times and get up eight every year in the classroom.

Publisher's Acknowledgments

Corwin would like to thank the following individuals for taking the time to provide their editorial insight and advice:

Scott Bailey
Principal
Waskom Middle School
Waskom, TX

Brian Bliss
Assistant Superintendent
Solanco School District
Quarryville, PA

Sue A. DeLay
Teacher—Math Interventionist
Oak Creek-Franklin Joint School District
Oak Creek, WI

Antwanette N. Hill
Director of Instruction
Hopper Middle School
Cypress, TX

Karen L. Tichy
Associate Superintendent for Instruction and Special Education
Catholic Education Office, Archdiocese of St. Louis
St. Louis, MO

About the Author

www.dailysphoto.com

Debbie Silver is truly a "teacher's teacher!" She is a former science teacher and an award-winning educator with 30 years of experience as a classroom teacher, staff development instructor, and university professor. Her numerous recognitions include being named the 1990 Louisiana State Teacher of the Year and the 2007 Distinguished Alumnus from the College of Education at Louisiana Tech University. Along the way, she has taught almost every grade level and most every kind of student.

Debbie is one of the most popular keynoters and professional development presenters in the United States. Audiences everywhere respond to her use of humor and sensitivity to remind them of how important teachers are in the lives of children. Her insights into student and teacher behavior are extraordinary. Through research-based theory, poignant stories, and hilarious characterizations, she connects with the souls of all who are involved in education.

Dr. Silver has been an invited author for several educational journals and has given keynotes at state, national, and international conferences in 49 states, throughout Canada, Europe, Mexico, the Middle East, and Asia.

Debbie is the author of the bestselling book *Drumming to the Beat of Different Marchers: Finding the Rhythm for Differentiated Learning*. She is a coauthor of *Because You Teach* and *Middle School Matters*. Songs she cowrote with Monte Selby are featured on his latest CDs. She and her husband, Dr. Lawrence Silver, have five grown sons, three daughters-in-law, and five grandchildren (so far). They live with two dogs in Melissa, Texas.

Debbie can be reached through her website: www.debbiesilver.com

Self-Motivation

What Is It and How Do We Use It to Empower Children?

. . . .

*What lies behind us and what lies in front of us are
but tiny matters as compared to what lies within us.*
—Ralph Waldo Emerson

. . . .

As a child, I was told, "Anything easily obtained is cheaply held." My parents were trying to tell me that that people don't usually value things that are just handed to them. They felt it was better to work for things you wanted. I think that maxim could also be stated as "Anything easily *attained* is cheaply held." I believe when children have to stretch themselves to master new learning they are more motivated and more appreciative of what they achieve. This chapter explores the nature of motivation and explains how teachers and parents can empower students by increasing their capacity for *self-motivation*. Motivated learners are willing to seek more learning, which is one of the requisites for being successful.

Self-motivation is severely damaged when learners experience a sense of *entitlement.* There is a growing concern about

1

the increasing manifestation of entitlement attitudes exhibited by many children in our nation today. "Entitlement" is the term used in this case to describe the belief that people have a right to happiness rather than the duty to construct it for themselves. It is the idea that people are endowed with the right to have certain benefits and material goods whether they have been earned. Brian Russell, a licensed psychologist; attorney-at-law; and familiar national television pundit on psychological, legal and cultural issues, states the following:

> Well-meaning parents are the foremost instillers and nurturers of entitlement attitudes. When they go beyond satisfying all of their children's needs and start satisfying all of the children's wants as well, these parents not only "spoil" the kids figuratively, but they also literally spoil the kids' chances of learning how to manage resources responsibly. When kids learn to expect excess rather than to anticipate scarcity, they learn to expect needs and wants to be satisfied equally rather than to differentiate and prioritize between and among them. They also learn to expect others to make sacrifices for them rather than to be self-reliant. (Russel, 2009, para. 3)

If in fact today's young people are more prone to feelings of entitlement than were their predecessors, what is the cause? *Wall Street Journal* writer Jeffrey Zaslow, in his article "The Entitlement Epidemic, Who's Really to Blame?" (2007), answers his question this way:

> **The self-esteem movement** [among others]. In 1986, California created a state task force on self-esteem. Schools nationwide later adopted "everybody's a winner" philosophies. One teacher told me that her superiors advised her to tell students that she liked their smiles, or the way they sat up straight, rather than focusing on, say, their failed spelling tests.

The *self-esteem movement* can be traced back to the 1970s. During that time, I was a parent and a teacher. I bought into the idea that helping kids feel good about themselves was the most important contribution I could make to their interests and, ultimately, to society's benefit. I have changed my mind about how I can best equip learners for a lifetime of successful living. I am convinced that neither I nor anyone else can inspire a child to be successful long term through superficial praise, external rewards, or a hesitance to give them accurate feedback.

Early in my teaching career, the trend was to build children's self-esteem by making sure everyone was a winner. The self-esteem movement is based on the belief that if we make kids feel good about themselves, despite their lack of accomplishment, their positive perceptions will translate into better schoolwork. We did everything we could to keep them from failing at anything. Sometimes, we curved grades, *dumbed down* the curriculum, and gave awards to everyone so that no one felt left out.

There is nothing wrong with wanting a person to feel better about himself. However, esteem needs to be attached to substantive accomplishments, courageous acts, extended insights, and the like. In the 1970s during one of our State Department of Education's programs to raise student self-esteem, I was given an array of activities to implement with my middle grade students. In one activity, I was directed to have them put their ink-covered thumbs on a piece of white poster board. After all the thumbprints were collected on the class poster, we were supposed to discuss the importance of individuality and then close by chanting, "I am 'thumb-body.'" My middle school students laughed aloud at the *lameness* (as they called it) of the exercise. I had to agree. It was pretty silly.

Not that all well-meaning attempts to raise student's self-esteem are ineffective, but I think some are tremendously misinformed. You cannot change a person's self-image long term with a one-shot motivational speaker, positive attitude posters, or by chanting, "I am thumb-body." Even a very powerful person in your life telling you that you are attractive, you are smart, you are talented, you are capable, and so on will not change your self-image very much or for very long. Rather than concerning ourselves with self-esteem, we would better serve our students with attention to *self-efficacy.*

Albert Bandura and Self-Efficacy

Albert Bandura (1997) introduced a psychological construct he calls *self-efficacy.* Through his research as a psychologist and researcher, he concluded that the foundation for human motivation is not just about believing one has certain qualities but rather that one believes she has power over her life. Self-efficacy beliefs provide the basis for human motivation because unless people believe they can affect changes in their circumstances and their lives, they have little incentive to act or to persevere through difficult situations.

Self-efficacy is unlike other qualities such as self-esteem because self-efficacy can differ greatly from one task or domain to another. A person may have very high self-efficacy about learning to Zumba dance and very low self-efficacy concerning learning trigonometry. It is also important to note that self-efficacy judgments are not necessarily related to an individual's actual ability to perform a task; rather, they are based on the person's beliefs about that ability.

Bandura (1997) speculates that people with high-perceived self-efficacy tend to feel they have more control over their environment and, therefore, experience less uncertainty. Individuals are more likely to select tasks and activities in which they feel competent and confident. They are apt to avoid those in which they do not feel that way. The higher the sense of self-efficacy, the greater the intrinsic motivation and effort people put toward their goals. They will pursue their course longer and with more diligence than will someone who is not self-efficacious. Research also clearly indicates that people with a highly evolved sense of self-efficacy recover from failure and setbacks more quickly than do those who do not.

Self-efficacy is bolstered when a student achieves something previously thought unattainable. Overcoming initial failure is a powerful incentive for further pursuits. We should provide students with numerous examples of ordinary people who have become extraordinary by overcoming failure repeatedly. We ought to model for them how to learn from missteps and how to stay true to their goals. We have to help students understand that their efforts and their choices make a tremendous difference in outcomes.

SELF-EFFICACY AFFECTS

- The **choices** we make
- The **effort** we put forth (how hard we try)
- Our **perseverance** (how long we persist when we confront obstacles)
- Our **resilience** (how quickly we recover from failure or setbacks)

Bandura believes that verbal persuasion may temporarily convince people they should try or should avoid some tasks, but finally, it is one's direct or "vicarious experience" with success or failure that will most strongly influence one's self-efficacy. He maintains that high degrees of self-efficacy are built over time and from many sources, but the most influential events that shape positive self-efficacy are mastery through purposeful effort. In later studies, Bandura demonstrates that people can learn from watching others they view as similar to themselves. Learning through viewing models is not as strong as mastery experience in helping create self-efficacy beliefs, but the effects of modeling can contribute to observers' beliefs about their capabilities (i.e., "If she can do it, so can I.").

Motivation or *Self-Motivation?*

It is a misnomer to say, "It is the teacher's job to motivate students." Motivation is not something we can give anyone or do to someone. It is not necessarily transferred from an enthusiastic adult to an uninspired student. The more accurate term to use is *self-motivation*. Self-motivation is what ignites a learner; it is the internal voice that says, "I am an autonomous person who has power over my choices and my actions. I can affect positive changes in my life if I work for them."

In 2000, Ryan and Deci concluded that if adults want to foster the most high-quality forms of enhanced performance, creativity, and persistence, they must design activities that give students a sense of autonomy, competence, and relatedness. They agree that the optimal state of self-motivation resides in the learner and must be fostered by the teacher. Oftentimes, a student's sense of entitlement is at cross-purposes with the awareness of self-motivation.

In working with educators and parents throughout the country, I sometimes hear the common question, "Kids today are so hard to motivate; what is wrong with them?" Typical complaints I hear from adults today are the following:

"My siblings and I could entertain ourselves with nothing but a can and a stick. Kids today are basically lazy, spoiled, and need to be constantly entertained!"

"My son gives up at the first sign of discouragement. It's like he thinks he can be the next Michael Jordan by just wishing it!"

"My child told me she didn't ask to be born—it was *my* choice. She acts like it is my responsibility to make sure she's not bored. Kids today are so self-absorbed."

"My students won't do their homework, and don't even think about asking them to do something hard! If it's not easy, they just quit."

"Our 12-year-old says he hates school because it is boring. If he had his way, he'd just stay in his room and play video games from morning to night."

Most parents and teachers yearn for students who are eager to learn new things. Some adults look hopefully toward the next advanced technical device or revolutionary new product that will make children *want* to learn. They wring their hands in frustration over what they consider unmotivated students.

Actually, the concept of the *unmotivated child* is an anomaly. Kids start out as interactive discoverers of the world and arc naturally curious explorers. Everyone has a basic desire for recognition and productivity. We are hardwired to enjoy achievement and to overcome obstacles in our paths. Consider the toddler who has just figured out she can open a kitchen cabinet and explore the contents within. She is quite resolute in her pursuit of removing pots and pans. Even if a saucepan lid lands heavily on her leg or if she scrapes her arm trying to push too close to the edge of the cabinet, she will continue her mission. She is determined and resolved. She approaches her undertaking with a tireless zeal. Any interference with her purposeful task by an outsider (e.g., Mom or Dad) will be met with vigorous objection and vocal displeasure. The child is self-motivated and wants to learn about this unexplored territory. Once all the objects that were previously neatly stored in the cabinet are displaced on the kitchen floor, she is off to conquer new worlds.

Think about the teenager yearning to drive a car. With all the talk about apathetic teens who seemingly cannot read well, communicate coherently, or even remember important homework assignments, is it not amazing how most of them are able to pass written and manual driver's tests? These same supposed slackers usually show up on time for and are able to pass a thorough written exam. If they fail it the first time, they voluntarily continue to take the test until they finally demonstrate enough mastery to move on to the performance assessment. For the next phase, they show up on time, use every cogent communication skill they can muster to talk with their examiner, and under extremely stressful conditions manage to maneuver the vehicle with enough proficiency to pass the final part of their test. Who does not remember the thrill and the pride of receiving that first driver's license?

Try This

Let's be clear about what we are talking about when I use the term self-motivation. I want you to think of something you have accomplished in the last few years—something important to you, something you really wanted to do. It can be a goal, an accomplishment, something you wanted to learn, something you wanted to win, or just something you wanted to finish. When you first thought about it, you may not have been very sure about whether you would be successful, but it is something you had to try for yourself.

(Okay, I see you trying to continue reading here without doing this exercise. Don't do that. Seriously, this will mean more to you if you stop and do this little mental exercise.)

Now picture the steps you had to take to attain your goal—the big ones and the little ones. Maybe your friends and family were on your side saying things such as this:

"I know you can do it."

"I'm here to help."

"You've got what it takes."

"Don't give up."

Or maybe they weren't so supportive. Maybe you heard things such as this:

"You've got to be dreaming."

"Don't you think that goal is a little ambitious for some-one like you?"

"You know you always have the great ideas, but you never follow through." (*You get the idea*).

The point is it really doesn't matter what *they* said or did. What matters is what *you* did to achieve your objective. You probably had to do some things you had never done before—take some risks, stretch your abilities, and work harder than you ever had before. And just as important, you had to give up some things—a safe zone, maybe some sleep, maybe some comforts. But in the process, you committed your heart and soul to the thing you wanted. You did whatever it took.

Do you remember how you felt the moment you realized it finally happened—when you had that one brief shining moment of realization that you *did* it? *You did it.* I wasn't there, but I'll bet you felt like putting your fists on your hips, sticking out your chest, and shouting a "TUH-Tuh-Tuh-DAH!" super-hero call.

TUH-Tuh-Tuh-DAH! for Kids

I'll bet you also felt like you could do more of the same thing you just did and were willing to try. Is there anything more gratifying for a child than to accomplish something that she was heretofore unable to attain? Think about the sheer joy for the girl when she puts her entire heart and soul into a directed effort. At first success evades her, but she continues to try new strategies, to patiently build a repertoire of skills until she finally makes it happen. Immediately the child gleefully proclaims, "I did it! I *did* it!" Then she often asks, "Did you see that?" Finally, she announces, "I did it all by myself!" Generally, at that point, the child is ready and more than willing to proceed to the next level.

That moment holds one of the greatest feelings in the entire world. And I want that feeling for all our children today. I want kids to have more TUH-Tuh-Tuh-DAH! moments in their school days and at home. My belief is that those moments can provide a carryover effect that keeps us moving forward through the moments that aren't so spectacular.

Unfortunately, in a world of enabled, entitled, protected offspring, we have robbed them of the very essence of what builds resilience, persistence, courage, patience, and joy. We rush in to make sure children feel good all the time. We don't want to risk getting their egos bruised or their comfort zones violated.

Moreover, we sometimes behave in ways that imply the only way to get kids to do anything taxing or responsible is to make them do it.

Amy Chua, Author of *Battle Hymn of the Tiger Mother*

Amy Chua, Yale law professor, recently created quite a controversy over her contention that her Chinese and other Eastern cultures do a much better job rearing children than do traditional Western parents. She contends that children never want to work hard on their own, so parents must force them to work hard now and learn to reap the rewards later. Although I agree with her view that there is an overreliance on self-esteem in the Western world, I disagree with her on the issue of whether children are intrinsically motivated. Behaviorists, in general, believe that the only way to get children to comply is to coerce them either overtly or covertly.

However, I have seen countless children work hard on their own, with virtually no input from an adult. I am old enough that when I was pregnant I did not know the sex of my unborn children. Sonograms had not yet reached their zenith in the rural area of Louisiana where I lived. I had two boys and was expecting a third baby. My nine-year-old and my six-year-old decided that if the new arrival was not of male origin, they would be forced to abandon our family forever. They devised a plan and enlisted their two best friends, also brothers, to pursue it. We lived on a 42-acre plot of wooded land etched by a tributary to a nearby river. The boys decided they would dig a pond near our backyard that would eventually connect to the creek leading to the river. Their plan was to build a raft capable of sailing them to the river, and if a female child was born, they would sail away, never to be heard from again.

I laughed when I heard their preposterous idea, but I figured even if they dug up some of the yard, it wouldn't matter. With no provocation or assistance from any adults, these two nine-year-olds and their six-year-old brothers began their labor of love. It was summer, so every day they were able to devote the full day to digging in the hard dirt. In Louisiana during the summer, the heat and the humidity are stifling, but the boys were undaunted. Filthy with grime and sweat, they paused only for food, refreshment, and other essential needs. They worked from sunrise to sunset every day for weeks. My oldest, usually the leader of the pack, devised a work schedule and a division of labor that would have delighted the Army Corps of Engineers. While two dug, two cut and stripped small saplings for the raft. They worked tirelessly. I began to worry when the hole reached proportions of about 100 square feet and a depth of three to four feet. But on they worked. I'm not sure how long this would have gone on, but eventually my third son was born, so the river project was moot, and the boys moved on to other endeavors. The hole they dug was so large that when it rained it really did create a pond of sorts, and they enjoyed the use of it for years. My point is that I have seldom seen children work as hard at anything in my entire life. Of their own volition, with their ingenuity, and without any adult meddling, these boys performed hour upon hour of backbreaking labor toward a goal they set for themselves. And they loved every minute of it. They were truly self-motivated. (TUH-Tuh-Tuh-DAH!)

I have watched children in skateboard areas try to master new techniques. They fall down. They get up and try again. They get scrapes and bruises and keep trying. They do the same moves over and over and over. They do not get bored, whine, or complain. They keep trying until they master the desired skill. TUH-Tuh-Tuh-DAH! They are truly self-motivated. Unlike Ms. Chua and other behaviorist advocates, I think children are naturally motivated to do many things.

Adults Need to Work in Tandem With Children's Motivation

I am not saying that children should be allowed to pursue only what interests them at the exact moment. Often, it is hard for them to see the big picture and understand the things they will need to attain mastery. They do not yet understand that some steps are really building blocks for future pursuits. I think part of the adult's job is to explain those things to children—to help them see relevance in their endeavors. I still maintain that children are intrinsically motivated, and with the proper kind of feedback, they can learn all sorts of necessary skills and self-sustaining learning practices.

I don't think the goal of most adults is to act as policing agents who enforce our desires on our reluctant subordinates. We would much prefer that children make wise choices, and we would like to be able to support their pursuit of them. We would rather not force kids to do things against their wills. So how do we set about capitalizing on what is already there—children's natural enthusiasm for becoming independent learners? How do we provide every child with more TUH-Tuh-Tuh-DAH moments? We need to examine purposefully how adults can foster that very special kind of motivation in our children as well as in ourselves.

Edward Deci, codeveloper of *self-determination theory* and a researcher who has expertise in intrinsic motivation, is convinced that children seek the novel and are eager to learn until adults get in the way:

> For young children, learning is a primary occupation; it is what they do naturally and with considerable intensity when they are not preoccupied with satisfying their hunger or dealing with their parents' demands. (1995, p. 19)

One might ask, "If children are so naturally inquisitive, what happens to their drive and enthusiasm as they grow older?" One explanation is that as individuals interact with their environment they take in all kinds of feedback. Their attempts to problem solve meet with varying degrees of success and failure. Individuals evaluate themselves, and they consider the responses of others in their lives, particularly important adults. All of the input shapes the individual's self-identity. Many times, the perceived self is quite different from the actual self, but growing research indicates people act more in accord with their self-perception than with reality.

Entitlement or Empowerment?

We need to shift our focus from doling out unmetered praise in hopes of raising their self-esteem to helping them understand the power they have in making positive choices and sustained efforts. We should worry less about entertaining kids and more about engaging them in meaningful tasks that encourage self-motivation. To help our young people feel the confidence of self-efficacy and empower them with resilience, we have to avoid filling them with an entitlement mentality. Next are some examples of how adults can begin this process.

Sample Adult Statements

Entitling: "You are all in the top math group, and this test is going to be a piece of cake for you. I know you are all going to make me proud by scoring higher than anyone in the state! Let me hear you say it, 'I am thumb-body!'"

Empowering: "You have shown tremendous growth in your math reasoning strategies this year. You have practiced some of the exact kinds of problems in class and successfully solved them. Just take your time and use the skills you have already mastered."

Entitling: "You won this tournament last year, and you are a shoo-in to win today. Your brother won this title two years in a row, and you will, too. Everybody knows you are a superstar!"

Empowering: "You are prepared, and you have done all the things needed to get you here today. You have demonstrated your athletic skills repeatedly in this game. You are likely to meet some fierce competition today, but you've done that before. Go out there and put your heart and your soul into it. Do your best, and let the rest take care of itself."

Entitling: "Well, since you are about the right age for one, we're going to let you get a puppy. But don't expect us to feed it or take care of it. That is going to be your job. If you don't do what you are supposed to, that dog goes back to the shelter. Do you hear me? I mean it."

Empowering: "You have shown your father and me that you can be responsible to do important tasks without being prompted. We have watched you play with the neighbor's dog and noticed how gentle and kind you are with her. We have decided you are someone who would make a reliable pet owner. Yes, you may have a puppy."

Entitling: "With your natural ability you are going to go far! You have more talent in your little finger than most other kids have in their entire bodies! This is effortless for you. You are going to be a superstar one day. That's for sure!"

Empowering: "You really seem to have a knack for this. And more important, you seem to love the craft. If you want to continue to improve, you're going to have to keep challenging yourself to work on all areas of your art. Keep practicing and stay focused. It will be fun to see how far you want to go with this."

Entitling: "I really can't afford to buy you those expensive sports shoes, but I don't want you to be the only kid in class who doesn't have them.

We'll get them, but I want you to take good care of them, okay?"

Empowering: "I certainly understand your desire to wear the same kind of shoes as the rest of your friends. However, I don't have that much money in my budget for clothing. Here's what I'll do. I'll give you the money I set back for shoes, and if you decide you want more expensive shoes, you can make up the difference with your money."

Entitling: "I'll be interested to see how you gifted-and-talented students do in the science fair. You all have what it takes to have the best projects ever. I'll be waiting anxiously to see your presentations in six weeks. I just know we are going to sweep the ribbons this year."

Empowering: "I've heard some very interesting ideas from you for your science fair projects. Great ideas are an important start, but remember that these projects also require a long-term commitment to the design, data collection, and final presentation. Be sure to pick a topic that interests you, and here's a checklist with timelines to guide you. If you start now, you will have enough time to do a thorough job on each phase. I'll be meeting with you each week to check on your progress and answer your questions."

These illustrations are certainly not exhaustive, but I think you get the idea. The onus for success must be put back where it belongs—within the control of the learner. With students, we need to do a better job of connecting outcomes to effort. Chapters 4 and 5 elaborate further on that concept. Chapter 2 explains the theory behind the idea of raising the bar for learners.

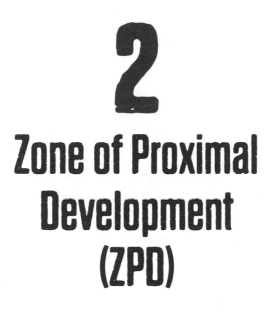

Zone of Proximal Development (ZPD)

Could something as simple as one theory provide the major underpinning for most motivational theory? Chapter 2 provides background, insight, and examples about one such theory, zone of proximal development. For students to have thriving futures, they must have self-motivation. For them to continue to recover from setbacks and failures, they must sometimes experience success that stretches them beyond their previous limits. Zone of proximal development (ZPD) can be used to accomplish both of these aims.

Mastery Learning Experience

The language arts teacher is monitoring a practice assignment she has given students to do in class.

Teacher: "Elan, you are not working on your assignment. Is there something you don't understand?"

Elan: "I don't get his part about writing two syn-o-some-things for each of the words on the list."

Teacher: "Okay, that word is pronounced 'syn-o-nym.' Do you know what that means?"

Elan: "No."

Teacher: "Well, let's start with something you do know. Last week, in class, we played Taboo, do you remember that?"

Elan: "Sort of."

Teacher: "In small groups you took turns trying to get your teammates to guess the word on the card you were holding, but you could not use terms that were listed as taboo, or off-limits."

Elan: "Oh yeah, Michael's team won. I remember now."

Teacher: "So when students were trying to get someone to say the word on their cards, what kinds of clues did they give?"

Elan: "Usually they named stuff that had something to do with the word on the card."

Teacher: "Yes, and what else?"

Elan: "Sometimes they used words that meant the same thing as the word on the card."

Teacher: "Okay, if I asked you to give me a word that meant the same thing, but was different from the word *furious*, what could you say?"

Elan: "I could say *mad*."

Teacher: "Anything else?"

Elan: "I could say *angry*."

Teacher: "Yes, I think I'd get it from those clues. Let's try different prompts this time." The teacher leads Elan through a series of examples and says, "I think you've got the idea." She then offers him a list of synonyms, anonyms, and homonyms and asks him to select the ones that mean the same thing. He gets most of them correct. The teacher explains the ones he misses.

Teacher: "So you obviously are able to recognize different words that mean basically the same thing. In Greek, the word *nym* stands for 'name,' and the word *syn* means 'the same.' Can you figure out what the Greek word *synonym* means?"

Elan: "The same name?"

Teacher: "Yes. And how does that relate to what we are doing today?"

Elan: "Oh! We are finding different words that name the same thing."

Teacher: "Yes, I think you've got it now. Look at your assignment and tell me what you are thinking for the first three examples." Elan successfully begins his assignment, and the teacher tells him to finish it on his own. She periodically checks on his progress and helps him make any necessary corrections. Later, she will help Elan discover that he can add power to his writing with the proper use of synonyms. Today, however, she silently celebrates that Elan learned something he did not know before; he had a mastery learning experience. TUH-Tuh-Tuh-DAH!

Parents and teachers have witnessed countless scenes like the one I just described. These are the fun moments. These are times teachers and parents feel delight in the roles we play in children's lives. We praise ourselves for deciding to have children instead of just cats or for entering the noble profession of teaching rather than taking that tempting job as a lighthouse keeper. But what about all of those times when children complain, avoid, deflect, and downright refuse to even try? How do we help them build self-efficacy when they stubbornly rebuff all efforts to get them to participate in tasks designed to help them learn? How do we compensate for their firmly held beliefs that they are dumb or untalented or so behind they can never catch up?

A common denominator I find among almost every motivational author and researcher is their emphasis on the importance of learners stretching toward consistently higher goals. They describe the necessity of pushing just beyond one's current state. Many describe the energized feeling people have when they are totally focused on an objective just beyond their present reach but within their perceived realm of possibility. These writers hold a common belief that the most powerful motivational reinforcer is for students to experience *earned success* (success they have had to work for). That is what I refer to as a TUH-Tuh-Tuh-DAH! moment. Nothing is more motivating than hard-earned success.

Lev Vygotsky and Zone of Proximal Development

In educational circles, most everything we are currently talking about regarding student engagement, achievement zone, optimal learning environment, learning zone, and the like can be attributed to the work of Russian psychologist and social constructivist Lev Vygotsky (1896–1934), who proposed a concept so fundamental to the theory of motivation that it undergirds nearly every aspect of its nature. In his research, he found that optimal motivation came for study subjects when they were asked to reach just beyond their present state but not beyond a reasonable expectation.

Vygotsky identified a student's zone of proximal development, or ZPD, as the rarefied area between a learner's current unassisted performance level and the point too far for a learner to presently reach (even with assistance). On the opposite ends of the continuum are the student's present level of comfortable mastery and the area totally beyond the student's level at the current time (see Figure 2.1).

Vygotsky, among other educational professionals, believes the role of education should be to provide children with experiences that are in their ZPD, thereby, encouraging and advancing their individual learning. The roles roughly resemble the following:

- Adult models the behavior for the student
- Student imitates the adult's behavior
- Adult fades out of instruction
- Adult offers feedback on students' performance

Figure 2.1   Zone of Proximal Development

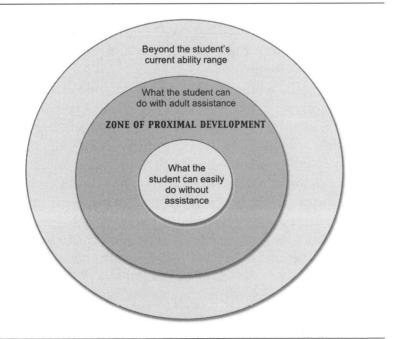

Scaffolding

Educators may be thinking, "Oh, that is where we must have gotten the idea of *scaffolding* that I hear so much about." Actually, Vygotsky never used that term himself, but others have since referred to "scaffolding" as the act of providing incremental stepping-stones to help learners move forward. Similar to erecting temporary platforms to facilitate movement higher and higher up a building, scaffolding in educational terms means figuratively to use helpful interventions to assist students in moving forward.

When differentiated instruction expert Carol Ann Tomlinson (2001, 2010) talks about "raising the level of support," she is basically talking about adults providing challenging but suitable steps for students to acquire requisite skills. Contrary to the concept of remediation, which generally refers to going back and doing something over, both scaffolding and raising the level of support suggest that instruction moves the learner forward rather than backward. Teachers should be able to break desired skills into logical parts and be attentive to things they can do to facilitate students in getting a foothold on the problem. Often, what is asked of students is not so much insurmountable as it is just too wide of a gap for them to span without the assistance of a skilled teacher.

Simply put, adults can maximize Vygotsky's ZPD as a strategic tool for helping students stay motivated toward a given task. The idea is to keep raising the bar just beyond the student's reach while giving only minimal support to make the leap to the next level. If we want to change our students' perceptions about themselves, we have to help them learn to accomplish goals. The bottom line is that mastering challenging goals produces true self-efficacy.

Educators and parents need to instruct students about purposeful practice and help them internalize the necessary mechanisms to reach just beyond their current grasps. Every learner deserves a reasonable chance at success, and working within a student's ZPD is a proven way to help every learner become self-motivated.

SCAFFOLDING INSTRUCTION GUIDELINES

Teachers can use many proven effective teaching strategies including the following:

1. Assessing accurately where the learner is in knowledge and experience

2. Relating content to what the learner already knows or can do

3. Giving examples of the desired outcome and/or showing the learner what the task *is* as opposed to what it *is not*

4. Breaking the larger outcome into smaller, achievable tasks with chances for feedback along the way

5. Giving students a chance to orally elaborate ("think out loud") their problem-solving techniques

6. Using appropriate verbal clues and prompts to assist students in accessing stored knowledge

7. Recognizing specific vocabulary that emerges from the exploration of the unit (emphasizing its meaning within the context of the lesson)

8. Regularly asking students to hypothesize or predict what is going to happen next

9. Giving students time and opportunity to explore deeper meanings and/or to relate the newly acquired knowledge to their lives

10. Providing time for students to debrief their learning journey and review what worked best for them

Basically, researchers agree that motivation functions most efficiently when the challenge is not too easy (boring) and not too hard (frustrating). In a 2010 presentation for the Association of Supervision and Curriculum Development (ASCD) Spring Conference, Carol Ann Tomlinson presented the following graphic representation (Figure 2.2) of what she calls zones of student feelings while working on a task. Her middle column, the achievement zone, gives excellent examples of what it might feel like to be working in one's ZPD.

So the task for teachers and parents is knowing our children well enough to gauge when and how much assistance they need. We must be mindful of where they are in their growth—not where they are *supposed* to be nor where we *wish* they were, but where they *really* are in their development. Then it is our job to break down the learning tasks into increasingly challenging, manageable steps. We model, we coach, and we keep moving the next step just beyond their

Figure 2.2 What Zone Am I?

Below	In	Beyond
I get it right away . . .	I know some things . . .	I don't know where to start . . .
I already know how . . .	I have to think . . .	I can't figure it out . . .
This is a cinch . . .	I have to work . . .	I'm spinning my wheels . . .
I'm sure to make out . . .	I have to persist . . .	I'm missing key skills . . .
I'm coasting . . .	I hit some walls . . .	I feel frustrated . . .
I feel relaxed . . .	I'm on my toes . . .	I feel angry . . .
I'm bored . . .	I have to regroup . . .	This makes no sense . . .
No big effort necessary . . .	I feel challenged . . .	Effort doesn't pay off . . .

The Achievement Zone

Source: Carol Ann Tomlinson, 2003. Used with permission. Retrieved from http://www.caroltomlinson.com/2010SpringASCD/Tomlinson_QualityDI.pdf

reach, where they can see it but have to stretch to reach it. Once the child masters a step, we are quick to remind them that they have just moved the starting point for next time. As coaches have always told their athletes, "If you can do it once, you can do it again."

A Very Simplified Illustration of ZPD

As a teacher, I often use simple examples to illustrate my points. As a presenter, I like to involve audience members in those illustrations. When I am talking about Vygotsky's ZPD, I remind audiences that effective coaches have always used the ZPD to help their players remain motivated. I set a chair in the middle of the stage. I draft some unsuspecting gentleman from the crowd and ask him to sit down. I tell him that I am the coach and he is my player. I ask for his last name since most of the coaches I know address their players only by their last names. It generally goes something like this:

Gruffly I say, "Wainwright, I want to know if you are left-footed or right-footed."

Wainwright replies, "Right-footed, sir."

"Okay," I growl, "I want you to stick your right leg out and up."

Wainwright obligingly sticks out his leg and lifts it somewhere around 12 inches off the floor.

I shake my head and scowl. "Put it down, son." I then put my hand on his shoulder, look him in the eye and say, "The operative word in that request was the word 'up.'" Pointing up I ask, "Do you know what 'up' means?"

He nods his head.

"Then please do me a favor and lift that leg UP!"

He lifts his leg higher this time, maybe 18 inches off the floor, and looks to me for approval.

Again, I shake my head and say, "Wainwright, I don't think you're hearing me. This task calls for you to get that leg of yours as high as you can possibly lift it. I frankly don't believe you are giving me everything you've got. I've watched you in practice, and I know what you can do. I don't know what's holding you back today, but you know. And I want you to do something about it."

I take his leg and hold it straight out and begin lifting it as high as I can. (Of course, the volunteer usually acts as if I am killing him at this point, and the audience roars.)

I squat down on one knee with my hand on his shoulder and look him directly in the eyes. "Son, I want you to put your heart and your soul in this. I want you to give this lift everything you've got. Don't hold back. Let's see what you are made of!"

Invariably, the volunteer will somehow manage to lift his leg almost twice as high as his original lift. I place my hand just beyond his toe and say, "Can you touch my hand with your foot?" He does, and the audience goes wild with applause, and the guy grins from ear to ear.

The audience laughs, and then I ask them, "Why did Wainwright's leg lift get higher each time?"

They respond with statements like "You had to show him what you meant." "You challenged him." "You kept 'raising the bar.'"

Then I say, "You're right about all of that. And here's the most important part. If I came back here next year to this same audience, brought Wainwright up on stage, and I told him to show us how high he can lift his right leg, how high will his first attempt be?"

There is a collective "ah" as several say, "He'll start at the highest point he reached today."

"Exactly," I tell them. "We just reset Wainwright's ZPD. As his coach, I would remind him repeatedly that he did it once, now he can do it again. And we would go from there."

In modeling successful life habits for students, we must help them learn to attain larger accomplishments through incremental steps. We can underscore the idea of *fall down seven times, get up eight* by constantly raising the bar just beyond their reach. Mastering new learning is one of the single-most effective ways to engage self-motivation. The following examples demonstrate how to use ZPD to empower students with necessary skills for success by giving them a challenging, but reasonable task.

ZPD Situations

Scenario

Ten-year-old Leo and his family frequently visit the lake during summer weekends. Leo complains that he wants to take his life jacket off while wading in the shallow end because he "looks like a dork" with it on. Dad decides it is way past time for his son to learn how to swim. Leo says he doesn't need to learn to swim because he's not planning on going into water that is over his head.

Beyond ZPD

Dad says, "Well, I'm tired of having to watch after you every minute, so you are going to learn to swim. I'm going to teach you the same way my father taught me." He removes Leo's life jacket and hurls him out into a deep part of the water. He then calls, "Okay, Leo, it's sink or swim time!"

(My dad actually did that to me, and I nearly drowned.)

Not Far Enough for ZPD

Dad tells Leo that learning to swim in the lake is too scary and hard. He assures Leo that he will take him to a swimming pool sometime and enroll him in a beginner's class. Leo objects saying that the beginner's class is for preschool kids, and he doesn't want to look like a baby. Dad agrees to let Leo take off his life jacket at the lake but insists that Leo stay within 3 feet of him all the time. Dad spends the entire day and subsequent visits following Leo around the shallow part of the lake.

Appropriate ZPD

Dad talks with Leo about how much they both enjoy visiting the lake. He engages him in a conversation about water safety and the importance of learning to swim. He tells Leo that he can wear a life jacket in and around the water or he can learn to swim. He assures Leo that he can take it one step at a time. He begins by having Leo practice putting his face in the water. He has his son rehearse moving his arms and legs to advance purposefully through the water. He gives Leo encouragement and feedback as he gradually introduces more swimming skills. When Leo is ready, Dad lets Leo remove his life jacket and monitors him as he practices swimming independently. Eventually, both Leo and his dad are better able to enjoy their visits to the lake.

• •

Scenario

Sola wants to be in the choir. Her music teacher is aware that Sola is not a strong singer. Her notes are often off-pitch, and she breathes at inappropriate times when she sings. Her vocal modulation is nonexistent, and she doesn't seem to be aware of it. She tells her choir director that everyone in her family tells her what a terrific singer she is and that she performs for family all the time. She questions the choir director's ability to know what good singing is. She announces that she plans to be on *American Idol* in a few years and would like to begin preparing now.

Beyond ZPD

The choir director invites Sola to join the tryouts for choir in front of her and two of her colleagues. The judges score the results and post the winners on the bulletin board. Sola's name is last on the list with the lowest points awarded. The choir director tells Sola that she might want to consider another avocation more suited to her strengths.

Not Enough ZPD

The choir director does not want to hurt Sola's feelings, so she invites her to sing in the choir. When the other choir members glare at her mistakes, she admonishes them to be friendly and not make Sola feel bad. She tries to give Sola lots of errands to run during choir practice so that she doesn't ruin the harmony, and she invites Sola to be her special student assistant director whenever there is a public performance so that Sola has another job to do instead of singing.

Appropriate ZPD

The choir director meets privately with Sola to determine if she is willing to put in the extra hours of practice it will take for her to be in choir. She records Sola's singing and plays it back to her along with recordings of some of her more accomplished peers. She helps Sola detect the differences in their performances. She assures Sola that anyone can learn to become a better singer with practice and with dedication. She and Sola develop a plan of action for Sola to meet her goals. She starts with beginning skills that Sola can practice at home and demonstrate to her teacher at school. Her choir director gives her candid feedback about her growth as a singer and gradually adds more technically difficult assignments for Sola to master. Over time, Sola is better able to blend with the choir, and she learns to ask for feedback from her friends about how to improve even more. She may never make it to the *American Idol* finals, but she will become a much better singer and a much more resilient learner because of the process.

• • • • • • • • • • • • • • • • • • • •

Scenario

Carlos and his siblings move from Mexico to the United States. His parents are determined to create a better life for their children in a new country. The family members speak limited English, but they want their children to attend the local school and do well there. They instruct their children to listen to their teachers and learn all they can. Carlos, the oldest, is enrolled in middle school, but he has not yet mastered the new language. He is a bit overwhelmed by the new town, the large school, and the very different way of life. He is quiet and eager to please and does not complain about the situation.

Beyond ZPD

Carlos's science teacher hands him a textbook, a course overview, a code of conduct, and a supply list. She tells him that he will need to bring his lab fee and a pocket folder by the next day. She believes that showing high expectations for him will be in his best interest, so she continues the lecture she started the day before and instructs him to take notes like the rest of the students. She assigns him a study guide to complete for the chapter and tells him the test will be on Friday. On Friday, she passes out the three-page multiple-choice test and gives the students 30-minutes to complete it.

At the end of the time, she picks up Carlos's test and notices that he only completed a small portion of the test. Later she puts an "F" on top of the paper and writes encouragingly, "You just need to study a little harder."

Not far enough for ZPD

Carlos's science teacher quickly ascertains that he is not working at grade level. She asks him several questions, and he seems confused. She does not want him to feel low self-esteem because he cannot do the work. She writes out a referral to the building level committee recommending him for special education. Eventually, Carlos is admitted for special services where he is given an elementary science book with lots of pictures. He spends most of his days doing cut-and-paste activities written several grade levels below his chronological age. He falls further and further behind his age group.

Appropriate ZPD

Carlos's science teacher welcomes him to the class and talks with him briefly to find out about his fluency with the English language as well as his background in science. She opens the textbook used in her class and asks Carlos to read a small section and explain the meaning of the passage. She observes that he struggles with the text and has difficulty making sense of it.

She smiles and tells him that while he is progressing with his proficiency in the English language there are other ways he can learn about science. She invites one of her bilingual students into their discussion. She tells Carlos that if at anytime during the discussion he is confused, he can ask Lily, the other student, to translate. She then opens the textbook and uses the pictures and graphics to explain the essential ideas the class has covered so far. She proceeds calmly and paces the instruction so that Carlos has a chance to think about the concepts in his first language as well as in English.

During the next few weeks, the teacher frequently monitors Carlos's understanding of the science concepts she wants him to master. She encourages him to use the phrases "More slowly, please" and "Please repeat" when he needs additional time to digest the information. She knows that it is best to pause after phrases or short sentences rather than after every word. She often loans Carlos a class iPod on which other students and adult volunteers have recorded the text the students are asked to read. Carlos is able to listen as well as to read the required print material.

In large-group presentations, the teacher uses broad gestures, sketches, photographs, and other visual materials to emphasize her points. She frequently does a quick recap with Carlos at the end of the class to help break information into smaller, manageable parts. She asks Carlos questions that require him to respond in phrases rather than with simple nods or headshakes.

For small-group work, she purposefully places him with Lily as well as two boys who have a passion for science and have demonstrated excellent interpersonal communication skills in the past. She often drops by their group to assess how they are doing.

When assessing Carlos, the science teacher tiers his test so that he is asked to respond to higher-order thinking skills with a minimum of rhetoric. Regularly, his tests are shorter and contain more visuals and graphics than traditional exams. She often provides Carlos with the opportunity to orally elaborate his understandings both directly to her and through free software on the computer called VoiceThread (www.voicethread .com). Until he masters both the language and the science concepts, Carlos is not given timed tests. He is allowed extra time to make sense of what is being asked. He is held to the same standards of science understanding as her other students, but the teacher supplies the level of support Carlos needs to have a reasonable chance at success.

Carlos progresses at or above the expected conceptual science understandings for his grade group while he continues to hone the skills of his new language. His teachers keep him moving forward without sacrificing essential understandings of the subjects they teach. They do not *dumb down* the curriculum nor compromise their expectations for Carlos, but they do provide the levels of support he needs to realize the success they all want for him. Carlos soon assimilates into his new learning community and sees himself as a capable learner.

Part of the preceding scenario actually happened to one of my former students (Carlos is not his real name). When he enrolled in his first school in the United States, he was placed in a special education program. Because of his still developing fluency and comprehension skills in English, the staff thought he had below-average intelligence and was incapable of handling grade-level work. He spent most of his day doing cut-and-paste activities, and he lived down to their low expectations. Thankfully, his parents were totally dissatisfied with this arrangement. They did not know what else to do, so they moved the entire family to another town in another state, which happened to be the small community where I lived and taught. Carlos was placed in regular education classes, and he had some exceptional teachers who recognized what he was truly able to do. I had the privilege of teaching him science one year, but at the time, I did not know about many of the teaching strategies I do now, and I did not use all the appropriate ZPD strategies listed previously. I did some things right but certainly not all that I now know to do. However, Carlos was a quick learner and one of the hardest workers I have ever known. He just needed a reasonable chance to be successful. As he assimilated into his grade group, it became obvious that he was exceptionally bright and determined. He graduated at the top of his high school class. In college, he remained on the dean's list every semester as he studied premedicine. He graduated from the Louisiana State University (LSU) Medical School and is now a successful practicing surgeon. He just needed a little scaffolding to get him headed in the right direction. (TUH-Tuh-Tuh-DAH!)

> *It is not reasonable to hold a student accountable for information presented solely in narrative he cannot read.*
> —Debbie Silver, EdD

ZPD plays a key role in helping students maintain self-motivation. Being required to reach just beyond one's current ability level creates a positive tension for learning, especially with a responsive adult monitoring the process. The theories of self-regulation and deliberate practice are also important to continual positive growth. Both of these ideas are discussed in Chapter 3.

Self-Regulation, Deliberate Practice, and Failure

That's what learning is, after all; not whether we lose the game, but how we lose and how we've changed because of it and what we take away from it that we never had before, to apply to other games. Losing, in a curious way, is winning.

—Richard Bach

Brian Russell (2009) believes the capability to delay gratification is "the ability that separates achievers from nonachievers in every society on Earth!" If that is true, helping students achieve proficiency with self-regulation is imperative to successful living. This chapter discusses the benefits of teaching students to postpone *instant gratification* for something more substantial and desirable in the long term. Dedicating themselves to deliberate practice and learning to overcome failure are two other essential components for the idea of fall down seven times, get up eight.

In his book *Crazy Busy,* Dr. Edward Hallowell (2007) describes our world as one of constant frenzy—a high-speed, high-tech world where our entire society is suffering from culturally induced ADD. He should know. Not only does he have ADD himself; he has also written a number of bestselling books on the topic. So in such a "crazy busy" world, how do we help our students master the art of self-control and purposeful choice? How do we build the essential elements of character that allow them to delay gratification when it is in their long-term best interests to do so? What are some ways we can inspire them to practice, especially those things they don't want to practice, with commitment and focus? How do we teach them that failure is a part of the growing process and does not need to halt their quest?

Instant Gratification and Its Implications

MISCHEL'S MARSHMALLOW STUDY

The Marshmallow Study, conducted in the 1972 by Stanford University psychology researcher Michael Mischel, demonstrated how important self-discipline is to lifelong success. He started his longitudinal study by offering a group of four-year-olds one marshmallow, but he told them that if they could wait for him to return after running an errand, they could have two marshmallows. The "errand" took about 15 minutes. The theory was that those children who could wait would demonstrate they had the ability to delay gratification and control impulse.

Study subjects had varying degrees of success with the task. Most were able to wait the entire period and receive two marshmallows, but some gave in at different time intervals and ate the marshmallow before the researcher returned. Mischel followed up with the subjects later and found the following:

12 to 14 Years Later
Those who waited for the two marshmallows (65%) were

- more socially competent,
- more personally effective,
- more self-assertive,
- better able to cope with life's frustrations,
- less likely to go to pieces under stress,
- less likely to become disorganized under pressure,
- more persistent in the face of difficulties,
- more self-reliant and confident,
- more trustworthy and dependable,
- more initiating and motivated with projects,
- still able to delay gratification in pursuit of goals,
- more academically successful,
- better at concentration and planning,
- more eager to learn, and
- earned 210 points higher scores on SATs.

Those who grabbed and ate the one marshmallow (35%) were

- socially introverted,
- more stubborn and indecisive,
- more easily upset by frustrations,
- more likely to think of themselves as "bad" or unworthy,
- more likely to regress or become immobilized by stress,
- more mistrustful and resentful about not getting enough,

(Continued)

(Continued)

- more prone to jealousy and envy,
- more likely to overreact to irritations with a sharp temper or provoking fights and arguments, and
- still unable to delay gratification or control impulses.

Source: Mischel, Shoda, & Peake, 1988.

In his classic study of delayed gratification, Mischel (Mischel, Shoda, & Rodriguez, 1989) recounts that he was not surprised by his immediate findings that 35% of his subjects had difficulty controlling their immediate impulse to eat the proffered marshmallow. He was, however, quite amazed to find that in a longitudinal study of many of the test subjects there was a significant correlation between the ability to delay gratification and the lack of successful adaptive behaviors later in life. The implications of that study are particularly important to parents and teachers who deal with children who are impetuous and lack self-discipline.

Dan Ariely (2011), writer for *Scientific American,* recently wrote on the subject of Mischel's studies and self-control, "Self-control may be something that we can tap into to make sweeping improvements [in] life outcomes" (para. 1). Many psychologists agree with him that children must be taught self-control; it is not something that is inherent.

Self-Regulation

Researchers often use the term "self-regulation" when discussing one's ability to postpone actions triggered by the body's basic needs of hunger, fear, thirst, distress, and the like. Many call this ability self-control. As individuals mature, we are better able to tolerate the distress that accompanies an unmet biological or psychological need by postponing or redirecting an inappropriate response (e.g., babies begin to wail the

TIPS FOR HELPING CHILDREN WITH IMPULSE CONTROL

- In class, do not allow students to raise hands or blurt answers. When asking for a response, require students to wait three to seven seconds before calling on someone randomly (I pick from a cup of craft sticks with the name of a different student on each one).
- Model "think-alouds" for students.

  1. The adult performs a task while thinking aloud. For example, "Before I start to do this activity, I need to read all the directions. After I read all the directions, I will check and make sure all the materials are here. Then I will begin with Step 1."

  2. The student performs the same task under the direction of the adult.

  3. The student performs the task while instructing herself aloud.

  4. The student whispers instructions to herself while doing the task.

  5. The student does the task while using "private speech."

- Teach students the "stop and think" five-step problem-solving strategy:

  1. What am I supposed to do? (Figure out what exactly what the problem is.)

  2. Look at all the possibilities. (Generate alternatives.)

  3. Focus in. (Try to shut out all environmental and mental distractions.)

(Continued)

(Continued)

4. Pick an answer. (Choose from the alternatives.)

5. Check out my answer. (Give myself credit if I'm right. If I'm not right, try to figure out how I made my mistake and what I can do next time that would be better.)

- Role-play with students the problems and possible solutions that occur in recurring social events.
- Use a timer to indicate periods of independent work and reinforce appropriate behavior with positive feedback.
- With defiant behavior, set a timer for one to two minutes. Tell the student he has a brief period to decide whether he wants to meet the terms of the request of the adult or take a consequence for his inappropriate choice.
- For younger children, the game Simon Says is an excellent reinforcement activity for thinking before acting.

moment they feel hunger, but older children generally are able to wait for the appropriate time to eat rather than to howl or grab the first available food).

In follow-up to his Marshmallow Study, Mischel and his research associates taught his subjects simple ways to avoid the temptation of eating the first marshmallow during the wait time. Among other things, he suggested the subjects pretend the marshmallow was really only a picture of a marshmallow with a frame around it and not a real tasty marshmallow. He was convinced that what we have historically called willpower is actually a matter of learning to circumvent basic primal messages from the brain.

In a 2009 *New Yorker* article, science writer Jonah Lehrer reported conversations he had with both Mischel and Angela

Lee Duckworth, an assistant professor of psychology at the University of Pennsylvania:

> According to Mischel, even the most mundane routines of childhood—such as not snacking before dinner, or saving up your allowance, or holding out until Christmas morning—are really sly exercises in cognitive training: we're teaching ourselves how to think so that we can outsmart our desires. But Mischel isn't satisfied with such an informal approach. "We should give marshmallows to every kindergartner," he says. "We should say, 'You see this marshmallow? You don't have to eat it. You can wait. Here's how.'" (para. 42)

Adults can help students learn to internalize self-regulation by modeling the behavior they want to see in children. Orally elaborating (thinking aloud about) one's choice emphasizes the conscious nature of taking control over the situation. Young people need to hear their mentors deal with the issue of delaying gratification so that they can emulate the behavior in their lives. Adults should purposefully articulate what they are thinking when they are making good decisions so that children understand everyone has to make conscious choices all the time. Here are some examples.

Adults Modeling Self-Regulation

Neutral Modeling: "We are not going to have this discussion in class now. The end."

Negative Modeling: "I'm so mad at you right now! I know I shouldn't be talking to you like this, but I am so angry I don't care! How dare you respond to me like that! I don't care if I get fired. I am going to tell you exactly how I feel about your profane language and your insulting remarks!"

Positive Modeling:	"Your response is inappropriate for this class. Right now, I am shocked by your outburst and feeling much too angry to deal with this in an effective way. I want to take a minute to calm down and clear my head. We will revisit this issue later after I have a chance to consider our options."
Neutral Modeling:	"No, I said I do not want a piece of cake. Period."
Negative Modeling:	"Oh, I'm aware I should say no to having a piece of cake, but I'm so hungry for something sweet I'm going to give in. I swear, I can resist anything but temptation. Ha-ha."
Positive Modeling:	"I'd like to have a piece of cake for dessert, but I know I won't make my goal weight if I continue to give in to temptation. I'm going to walk away from the table to avoid looking at and smelling that sugary delight any longer. I'll be much happier in the morning when I step on the scale if I say no to the cake for now.
Neutral Modeling:	"The principal has asked that teachers not drink sodas in front of students."
Negative Modeling:	"The principal has a new rule about teachers not drinking sodas in front of students. That's about the stupidest thing I ever heard of. She can't tell adults what we can and can't do. I'm going to put my soda in a different container so she won't know what it is. You kids tell me if you see her coming, okay?

Positive Modeling:	"The reason I'm not drinking soda in class anymore is that our administration thinks it provides a bad example for students. It's going to be tough for me to give up that habit, but I'll probably be better off drinking water anyway. If you see me walk in here with a soda, please remind me to get rid of it. It's important that all of us, even teachers, follow school rules."
Neutral Modeling:	"Your mother wants me to mow the lawn. I guess that's what I need to do."
Negative Modeling:	"Your mother wants me to mow the lawn, but I don't feel like mowing the lawn right now. Maybe I can distract her so she'll forget about asking me. I hate to mow the lawn, and she knows it. I'm going to fake a phone call from a friend so I can get out of mowing today."
Positive Modeling:	"Your mother just reminded me the lawn needs mowing. Mowing the lawn is not one of my favorite things to do, but I know that's one of my contributions to our family. Besides, the sooner I start, the sooner I'll finish. I think I'll try a new technique today just to make it more interesting for me. I may even try cutting a few designs into the grass before I even everything out. That will be fun; maybe I'll take pictures of my grass art."

Magic Words

Two words a parent or a teacher can say to the child struggling with self-regulation can sometimes work miracles. When the learner becomes disconsolate over being placed in a group she doesn't like or is faced with doing a particular classroom task she disfavors or is given a set of guidelines she finds obtrusive, this phrase can help alleviate the pain. What are these words with mystical proportion? "For now." Most students can deal with temporary situations if they know there is a time limit on them. When I tell the students we are going to do group work and get the eye roll from a student who hates cooperative learning, I say, "This is what we're going to do for now. It's not forever, not for the rest of the year, not even for the rest of the week—it's for now. Soon you'll have the opportunity to choose something else, but we're going to work in groups for now."

The magic words can be put to good use in trying to kick off a dreaded project. "Okay, let's just get this started for now." They can be used to halt a verbal confrontation: "The two of you need to step away from each other and totally ignore each other for now." They can even be used by adults struggling to keep their emotions in check: "Your body language tells me you are not ready to work this out yet. Let's put the issue aside for now and agree to talk about it later."

Even younger children can be appeased when we assure them that putting on dress-up clothes is just for now. "For later we can get back in our shorts and sneakers, but for now we are going to be dressed up." I generally try to provide a good reason for my decisions, whatever they are, but I leave no doubt about the declaration. Adults need to be assertive, but using the magic words can temper the impact of disagreeable situations for most children.

There's a freedom in those two words that assures learners we are not forgetting their needs and preferences. The words "for now" tell them we take note of their objections, and they also let them know the adult is ultimately the one in charge.

Why Is Practice So Important?

Self-regulation also plays an important part in pursuing a goal with tremendous effort as well as appreciating incremental progress toward success. Clearly, we all want students to develop the tenacity to pursue long-term goals even after the initial enthusiasm has left them. We want them to have the self-efficacy and the self-control to pursue their objectives in face of setbacks. But in today's *instant gratification society*, how do we promote that?

One of the biggest complaints I hear from parents and teachers is that students want *instant success* and *immediate fulfillment* without appreciating the value of determination, perseverance, or even practice. Geoff Colvin (2008), senior editor of *Fortune* magazine, wrote a book titled *Talent Is Overrated: What "Really" Separates World-Class Performers From Everybody Else*. In it, he debunks the idea that superstars are inherently more gifted, more talented, more physically suited, or necessarily smarter than anyone else. He cites example after example of ordinary people who became extraordinary through focused attention, deliberate practice, and a dedicated passion for their pursuits.

Malcom Gladwell's (2008) book *Outliers* and Matthew Syed's (2010) book *Bounce* make the same assertions. While Gladwell hedges a bit by talking about how important it is to "be in the right place at the right time," he also points out the need for deliberate practice and infinite dedication. Syed, who is an Olympic table tennis champion and sports journalist, details his life story about how he became a world-class player by following the tenets of intentional, purposeful practice.

All three of the aforementioned journalists agree that physical limitations sometimes do play a role in whether a person can excel in his field. (When is the last time you saw a 6'5" jockey, a 4'5" NBA player, or a 110-pound Sumo wrestler?) But the authors agree that most people are limited not as much by their physical or mental stature as by their unwillingness to give everything they have to achieving excellence. All three lament the fact that the "talent myth" often disenfranchises many who could be successful if they pursued their goals in a wholehearted, purposeful manner.

Colvin (2008), Gladwell (2008), and Syed (2010) mention similar anecdotal evidence observing that most perceived prodigies actually just had much more deliberate practice, usually at an early age, than did nonsuperstars in their respective fields (e.g., Tiger Woods, Mozart, Picasso, Thomas Edison, Venus Williams, Wayne Gretzky, Bobby Fischer, the Beatles). They all cite the same empirical research of K. Anders Ericsson to back their arguments.

Ericsson's Deliberate Practice

Dr. Ericsson is a professor of psychology at Florida State University. He is recognized as one of the world's leading theoretical and experimental researchers on expertise. Ericsson's (Ericsson, Krampe, & Tesch-Romer, 1993) studies with other researchers have yielded important information about the nature of excellence and expertise. He and his colleagues believe what is required of athletes, professionals, or others who desire to become expert in their chosen areas is what they term "deliberate practice." They define deliberate practice as an activity specifically designed to improve performance, often with the teacher's help. The task must be repeated many times. Feedback on results is continuously available, and the practice is highly challenging mentally. Whether the pursuit is intellectual or physical, deliberate practice is highly demanding and not a lot of fun. Ericsson says,

> Expert [deliberate] practice is different. It entails considerable, specific, and sustained efforts to do something you can't do well—or even at all. Research across domains shows that it is only by working at what you can't do that you turn into the expert you want to become. (Ericsson et al., 1993, p. 368)

As mentioned in Chapter 2, it is the adult's job to give a clear, unbiased view of the performance while asking the learner to stretch beyond her current abilities. Choosing aspects of performance to practice is an important skill. Learners can never make progress in their *comfort zones,* the innermost circle on Figure 2.1, because those activities are already done easily and require no growth. Activities in the *panic zone,* the outermost layer of Zone of Proximal Development (ZPD) chart, are so hard learners don't even know how to approach them.

Ericsson (Ericsson et al., 1993) believes that one should identify the "learning zone" (similar to Vygotsky's ZPD) and try to force oneself to stay continually in it as it expands. High repetition is an essential part of the process. Expertise comes when the learner begins to do things automatically without having to think through every step. This *automaticity* frees her mind to deal with higher-order tasks. Researchers believe that deliberate practice is transformative both physically and psychologically.

One of the consequences of overindulging children by letting them skip or shortchange practice sessions is that they stop getting better. They either learn to take shortcuts, which are nonproductive in the end, or they give up all together. Most children will practice more diligently and much longer if they have an attentive adult who gives them effective, specific feedback about how to improve. It helps to show them definitive evidence of their progress, no matter how slowly or how little it moves forward.

In a Nike "No Excuses" ad, Michael Jordan says,

> Maybe it's my fault. Maybe I led you to believe it was easy, when it wasn't. Maybe I made you think my highlights started at the free throw line, and not in the gym. Maybe I made you think that every shot I took was a game winner—that my game was built on flash and not fire. Maybe it's my fault you didn't see that failure gave me strength—that my pain was my motivation. Maybe I led you to believe that basketball was a God-given gift and not something I worked for—every single day of my life! Maybe I destroyed the game. Or maybe, you're just making excuses. (Nike, 2008b)

Jordan puts the responsibility for success squarely on the shoulders of those who need it—the players who want to "be like Mike!"

Expertise and the Ten-Year Rule

Students need to be aware of what it takes to be an expert at anything. In *Outliers,* Gladwell (2008) calls it the "ten thousand hours of practice" rule. He states that no one can reach excellence without that much deliberate practice. Ericsson's (Ericsson et al., 1993) studies referred to this same principal as the "ten-year rule." Since most deliberate practice requires about 1,000 hours per year, they are saying the same thing. It is important that adults tell students the truth about what it takes to reach the top. Students are inundated with so-called reality TV instant success stories, but these stories are greatly exaggerated or simply not true. Ericsson calls it the "iceberg illusion." He explains that it is what we see of an iceberg is only the top portion, or the tip, and the rest is literally a hidden mountain of ice. When we witness extraordinary feats, we are usually witnessing the product of a process measured in years of dedicated practice.

Adults need to have conversations about progress (fast or slow) with kids. Parents and teachers should take every opportunity to point out the intentional, purposeful practice it takes to get better at anything. Often, students are discouraged if they are not immediately successful or if they fail to make progress as quickly as they would like. It is helpful to share stories with them about people who started a little more slowly than their peers but who continued to work and push until eventually they surpassed the "quick starters" and "early bloomers."

Adults need to articulate to youngsters about our struggles and detours we took to get where we wanted and needed to be. Certainly, it is a lot more fun to do those things over and over that are easy for us, but we cannot grow from that. Meticulously examining our weak spots, getting appropriate feedback, and practicing those things that need improvement are requisite steps for fulfilling our dreams.

In his book *Drive: The Surprising Truth About What Motivates Us*, Daniel Pink (2009) also mentions deliberate practice to attain mastery. He describes it this way:

STEPS IN DELIBERATE PRACTICE

- **Remember that deliberate practice has one objective: to improve performance.** "People who play tennis once a week for years don't get any better if they do the same thing each time," Ericsson has said. "Deliberate practice is about changing your performance, setting new goals and straining yourself to reach a bit higher each time."
- **Repeat, repeat, repeat.** Repetition matters. Basketball greats don't shoot ten free throws at the end of team practice; they shoot five hundred.
- **Seek constant, critical feedback.** If you don't know how you're doing, you won't know what to improve.
- **Focus ruthlessly on where you need help.** While many of us work on what we're already good at, says Ericsson, "those who get better work on their weaknesses."
- **Prepare for the process to be mentally and physically exhausting.** That's why so few people commit to it, but that's why it works. (Pink, 2009, p. 159)

In his book *Bounce,* Matthew Syed (2010) makes a significant argument about how important practice really is:

The talent theory of expertise is not merely flawed in theory; it is insidious in practice, robbing individuals and institutions of the motivation to change themselves and society. Even if we can't bring ourselves to embrace the idea that expertise is ultimately about the quality and quantity of practice, can't we accept that practice is far more significant than previously thought? That talent is a largely defunct concept? That each and every one of us has the potential to tread the path to excellence? (p. 112)

Failure? There's an "App" for That

A large component of deliberate practice is to focus on one's weakest areas—areas of failure, so to speak. No one likes to fail, but failure is inevitable when one is attempting to learn new things. Failure is often treated as a state of being rather than as a temporary roadblock. Students and the adults in their lives often want them to avoid defeat at all costs. The Nike Company has another positive ad campaign that encourages people not to give up. In one spot Michael Jordan says,

> I've missed more than 9,000 shots in my career. I've lost almost 300 games. Twenty-six times, I've been trusted to take the game winning shot and missed. I've failed over and over and over again in my life. And that is why I succeed. (Nike, 2008a)

That's a powerful message for a superstar athlete to tell kids. Most of us have our stories of personal struggles we could and should share with students.

My Skating Rink Story

I learned an important lesson about failure when I was about nine years old. My one sport at which I excelled was roller-skating. I took a basic roller-skating course at the local rink to earn a Girl Scout badge. I was thrilled by the idea of moving around on wheels (back when each skate had four wheels, two in the front and two in the back). I seemed to have quite a knack for staying upright as I tried different feats, so I got interested in getting even better. After my lesson each Saturday with the other Girl Scouts, I would go home, clean out our garage, and practice relentlessly with my cheap little metal clip-on skates.

I spent hours and hours perfecting the moves I had been taught at the rink.

When I returned for my lesson each week, I was always one of the most proficient skaters. My success prompted me to practice even more. I was in a state of bliss. No one had to remind me to practice. I relished in the joy of learning new turns, jumps, and spins.

Of course, I enjoyed having my skating coach and people at the rink make a big deal about how good I was. Being the ultimate show-off, I thrived on getting better and better to prove what I could do. Very few of my classmates at school had any idea about the skills I had developed over the year. I was eager for our end-of-the-year school party at the rink so that I could show everyone, particularly the "mean girls," what a magnificent little skater I was. The day of the party came. I put on my skating skirt, tights, and boot covers. I entered the rink and attempted to marvel everyone with my prowess. Several of my close friends were excited about what I was doing and urged me to do more. I attempted to do several things I had barely learned, and I ended up in a heap on the floor. That didn't concern me. I'd hop right back up and start over.

At the end of the party, I was so pleased with myself. I thought I was due for at least a "Way to go, girl!" from my classmates. However, a few of the mean girls skated up to me and said, "We know you think you're a hotshot skater, but you're not. You fell down almost more than anyone here. The best skaters are the ones who don't fall down. You're not one of them!"

I was crushed. I felt like such a loser. As I was turning in my rink skates, my coach happened by and saw my tears. He asked me what was wrong. I told him that I felt like such a failure because I had fallen down so many times in front of my classmates, and now they were laughing at me.

He picked up my chin and looked right into my eyes. "Why do you care what they think, Debbie? Are you going to let a few snotty kids take away your joy in doing what you love? And let's talk about that falling down part. You have what I look for in every skater—a lack of fear to try new things. Of course, you fall down, but that's not failing, it's just falling! It's the only way you'll ever learn to do new things. You listen to me, young lady, any time you spend an entire session without falling down, you have wasted your time. Those bumps and bruises on your arms and legs tell me that you are always pushing a little harder, and that's what I call success!"

As an adult, I often look at my bumps and bruises (both the visible ones and ones that don't show) as my badges of honor. The old saying "Nothing ventured, nothing gained" is absolutely true. I don't like falling down any more than the next person, but I've learned to see the stumbles as part of the dance. I think we have to teach children that falling down is just a part of the process; getting up and trying again is what's important.

Helping Kids Deal With Failure

When students complain about failing, we should counter with this response: "Okay, you don't like the way that turned out. What did you learn from the experience?" Celebrating failure seems a bit simplistic and counterintuitive, but what we can learn to do is treat it as a normal aspect of growth. It's important for learners to grab onto something they can take away from every effort so that they can improve the next time they make an attempt. We should model for them how to learn from missteps and how to stay true to their goals.

Adults can emphasize the fact that failure is just a natural part of the learning process; we can model appropriate responses to temporary setbacks or roadblocks. We need to teach students about deliberate practice and help them understand that they cannot grow without some risk and some pain (physical and/or cognitive and/or emotional.) We have to empower them with the knowledge that their efforts and their choices are things they can control every day.

If we want children to internalize the desirability of the philosophy, fall down seven times, get up eight, it is important that we act as role models who incorporate this belief system into our daily lives. We need to verbalize it when we do it and call attention to our intentional choices to stand once again rather than give up.

For students to learn the important life lessons about perseverance and resilience, they need both modeling and practice. We need to ensure that both parents and teachers provide excellent standards for successfully handling setbacks and failures. The following are a few examples.

Adults Modeling Recovery Practices

Negative Modeling: "I am the world's worst cook! Every time I try a new recipe, I manage to find a way to ruin it. Look at that cake I made. Have you ever seen anything so pathetic? It looks like the Leaning Tower of Pisa! That's it. It probably tastes as bad as it looks. I'm tired of wasting money on stuff that ends up tasting like cardboard anyway. If you kids want a home-cooked meal, you're just going to have to wait for Grandma to visit."

Positive Modeling: "Okay, that cake could use a little structural support, but I'm hoping it will taste okay. I seem to always have trouble when I try a new recipe. Maybe I need to slow down and make sure I'm following the directions exactly. I think I'll start double-checking myself. Also, I'm going to check out one of those cooking DVDs from the library. Maybe if I could watch a master cook do the same things I'm trying to do, it would help. I'm really more of a visual learner, and watching others is how I learn best. Do you kids have any other ideas about how I can become a better cook?

Negative Modeling:	"Well, I didn't get that promotion I wanted. I was sure I was going to get it. I cannot for the life of me understand how Teresa got that job over me. I work harder than anyone on this staff, and does anyone really care? Obviously, they don't! That's it for me. I'm done. I never want to get my hopes up like that again."
Positive Modeling:	"Well, I didn't get that promotion I wanted. Apparently, they were looking for something they didn't see in me. The first thing I need to do is find out exactly what the administration is looking for when they advance people in the system. Then I'll need to try to improve whatever skills I'm lacking. I know I can do this. It's just going to take a little more time than I thought."

Committing to deliberate practice is hard for almost everyone. It is especially difficult for young people who don't always see the whole picture. It is much easier to keep doing what we have already mastered and feel competent about, but that is not how we grow. Self-regulation is a vital component to building the kind of character that compels us to keep at something long after our initial interest has left us and to keep pushing our limits far beyond what we previously thought they were. Self-regulation allows us to override our natural desire for a steady diet of victory and to begin to appreciate the lessons to be learned from failing. Being able to apply the lessons learned from our shortfalls is a key strategy to lifetime success. This topic is discussed further in Chapter 5.

> *Most people have the will to win, few have the will to prepare to win.*
>
> —Vince Lombardi

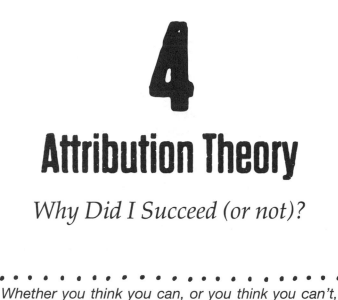

Attribution Theory

Why Did I Succeed (or not)?

. . . .
*Whether you think you can, or you think you can't,
you're probably right.*

—Henry Ford
. . . .

For years, parents and teachers have tried to foster a positive *can-do* attitude in kids by heaping praise on them. We thought bombarding them with "you're so smart" and "this should be easy for you" would bolster their egos and make them fearless. It may seem incongruous, but many theorists believe this type of inappropriate praise can do more harm than good. Adults can compellingly impact student self-efficacy with the nature of their feedback, and they should start by focusing on things the child can control. Chapter 4 probes the social psychology of attribution theory and how it is connected to promoting accountable, responsible, lifelong learners.

A SIMPLIFIED VERSION OF ATTRIBUTION THEORY

The teacher is monitoring her elementary students as they create a landscape drawing. Her eyes fall on Vincent's work, which is way beyond her wildest expectations for this age group. She feels she must comment.

"Why, Vincent, that is the most incredible landscape drawing I have ever seen from someone your age. How did you get that good at drawing? Oh, I know, your mom is a professional artist. I forgot about that. You must have inherited her genes. And I just remembered that your dad teaches art at the junior college. He must have given you a lot of direction in learning to draw. You are one lucky little guy, Vincent. No wonder you are so good.

"You know I never could draw. I'm a horrible artist. From now on when I need something illustrated on the board, would you do it for me? You really have the gift. You are now the official Class Artist. Way to go, Vincent."

She looks up to see everyone else has stopped working and is staring at her. She quickly smiles and asks, "Now which of you is ready to show *your* picture?"

Sometimes in workshops, I model the previous scenario. When I ask the last question, the audience usually breaks into laughter. They tell me there is no way they are going to try to compete with Vincent's work. I pretend to be quite shocked by their reaction. I tell them I was merely praising one of my students and ask them how that could possibly be a negative influence. On face value, it seems the teacher is complimenting Vincent, but the choice of her words is actually undermining both his and his classmates' motivation. To demonstrate how inappropriate praise can do more harm than good, let's look at the *theory of attribution.*

An important aspect to a mastery learning experience is a psychological concept termed attribution theory. Fritz Heider first introduced the idea in 1958 to describe the reasons people give for their success or lack of success on certain tasks. Later, Bernard Weiner (1979, 1980) asked subjects why they were or were not able to achieve certain goals. He recorded all their responses. He was able to sort the participants' responses into what later was classified as one of four groups:

ATTRIBUTION THEORY

- **Task Difficulty** (e.g., "The test was too hard." "I can't do a job like that. I'm just thirteen!" "That assignment was way easy.")
- **Luck** (e.g., "I was in the right place at the right time." "I guessed correctly about what to study." "I got stuck with the mean teacher this time.")
- **Innate Ability or Talent** (e.g., "I'm just good at math." "Being good at sports just runs in my family." "I can't dance—never could and never will.")
- **Effort** (e.g., "I studied really hard, and I was prepared this time." "I waited until the last minute to study." "I didn't put the time on this assignment I needed to.")

The interesting thing about attribution theory is that it incorporates the major tenets of self-efficacy, self-regulation, and cognitive theory. It is deceptively simple, and yet it is the cornerstone for self-motivation. Students generally have explanatory assumptions about why they are or they are not successful, and those ideas are usually tempered by their view of themselves in the world.

Look again at the four categories listed previously. They represent the primary causal factors cited by individuals as explanations for their success or failure on certain tasks. Three of the four of these have something in common that should be particularly significant for teachers and parents. Do you see it?

The first three attributions are all beyond the control of the learner. They are external factors that cannot be influenced by the student. If learners attribute their success or their lack of it to one of the first three factors, they are basically giving up their *locus of control* (their belief that they have power over what happens to them). The singular attribute a student can influence is the fourth one, *effort.* Effort is the only factor that can be controlled by the learner. The ramifications of this research are astounding. When parents and teachers praise innate talent and/or luck, we diminish the student's role in his success. If we allow kids to dismiss their low achievement because of the task difficulty or other external factors, we are complicit in letting them off the hook. After all, they cannot control their genetic makeup, fate, or how hard or how easy the undertaking is. What is important about attribution theory is that adults can use it to help children accept responsibility for their successes and failures. Students can learn how to empower themselves rather than feel entitled or victimized.

More on A Simplified Version of Attribution Theory

In the opening scenario, the teacher praised Vincent's art, but her words undercut everyone's sense of internal control. She implied the only way to be successful on that particular assignment was to have "good genes" and/or be lucky enough to have a parent who teaches art. In a subtle but powerful way, she gave every other student permission to stop trying. ("Well, my mom's not an artist, so I might as well quit." "I can never draw like Vincent so why even try?")

How many times have we heard struggling learners moan a complaint such as these: "I can't do that assignment because I'm not smart like he is!" "I'm not good at sports like she is; I hate this game." "I made a bad grade because I got the tough teacher." "I failed because that test was way too hard." When we allow students to say those things (or, worse, when we say those kinds of things to them), we are teaching them they are powerless over their lives.

Learned Helplessness

In the example of the art teacher's comments, consider what she said about herself. She said that she is not a very good artist. She wants Vincent to take over all the future drawing for her. In essence, she just modeled for the class the following idea: "If I doubt my abilities, I will just get someone else to do it for me."

Occasionally, in class, I have students who remind me of Eeyore, the gloomy little donkey from the Winnie-the-Pooh stories. Like Eeyore with his perennial "Oh, nooooo," they are passive, pessimistic, and disconsolate; they always seem to expect the worst. My efforts to cheer them up are either rejected or ignored completely. And while I also know adults with similar dispositions, it is far more unsettling for me to witness this hopeless attitude in kids. I have come to realize that some children suffer from an extreme version of negative attribution known as *learned helplessness.*

Learned helplessness is a dysfunctional condition that is generally associated with students who have very low self-efficacy and are unable to cope with requirements for academic or social success. These students believe they have no control over unpleasant things that happen to them. As underachievers, they often show symptoms such as persistent failure, lack of motivation, avoidance, inability to concentrate, reluctance to try, and apathy bordering on depression. Educational diagnostician Carmen Reyes (2011a) believes that children with learning disabilities are particularly prone to this condition:

Learned helplessness seems to contribute to the school failure experienced by many students with a learning disability. In a never-ending cycle, children with a learning disability frequently experience school difficulties over an extended period, and across a variety of tasks, school settings, and teachers, which in turn reinforces the child's feeling of being helpless. (para. 3)

The phrase "learned helplessness" literally means one has learned to view the world with a victim mentality. The term was originated by Martin Seligman (1975) from his research studies with Steve Maier at the University of Pennsylvania in 1965. They used dogs in an experimental study about learned behavior. Experimental dogs were classically conditioned with indiscriminant electrical shocks over which they (the dogs) had no power. Later, when given the opportunity to escape the shocks they made no attempt to do so. The conditioned dogs were placed in a box divided into two sections by a low barrier. Because only one side of the box was electrified, the dogs could easily have avoided electrical shocks by hopping to the other side. Unlike the control-group dogs who immediately hopped into the side with no shocks, the conditioned dogs just stayed in the electrified side, feeling helpless to change the situation. They simply laid down and whimpered rather than trying to free themselves. Seligman surmised that the dogs had basically learned to be helpless.

Similar experiments using irritating noises rather than shocks were subsequently tried with people. Seligman later extended his research to work with migrants, the poor, minorities, and other socially disenfranchised groups. Surprisingly, though, researchers found that occasionally the conditioned humans did not simply endure their fate, but rather tried to do something about it.

Seligman (2006) recognized that some people have very different reactions to the same situations that lead others into a state of learned helplessness. He theorized that a person's attribution style is the key to understanding why some subjects respond dissimilarly to adverse events. Although a particular individual may experience the same or similar negative events, how each person privately interprets or explains the event will affect the likelihood of acquiring learned helplessness (e.g., after a disaster, some people see it as an unfortunate incident and will immediately start rebuilding their lives exhibiting hope and optimism. Others may see the event as a personal assault and be totally debilitated and no longer able to attend to even the most basic essentials for living.)

Seligman (2006) uses these new findings to make a case for another construct he calls *learned optimism,* which he says can be facilitated by one's healthy use of attribution theory. He stresses that because maladaptive reasoning behaviors are learned, they can be *un*learned.

Working With Learned Helplessness

An important point emphasized by Reyes (2011b) is that children with a sense of learned helplessness do not necessarily lack requisite skills or ability. Rather, it is their perception of themselves that is flawed. Those of us who work with kids know that for them perception *is* reality. A child who is convinced he is incapable or unworthy will not be swayed by mere compliments, cajoling, or lectures on self-esteem. Children need to see clearly the connection between their efforts and school success. Children who perceive this connection are more likely to avoid learned helplessness (Ames, 1990). Thankfully, there are proactive measures adults can use to help students *un*learn helpless behavior.

STRATEGIES TO COMBAT LEARNED HELPLESSNESS

1. **Help students understand that everyone has problems, fears, failures, and self-doubt. Share stories about people like those who have overcome similar or even harsher circumstances.**

   Dr. Mel Levine has written two outstanding books for students on the topics of learning disabilities: All Kinds of Minds: A Young Student's Book About Learning Abilities and Learning Disorders

   (Continued)

(Continued)

(1990; for younger students) and Keeping a Head in School: A Student's Book About Learning Abilities and Learning Disorders *(1992; for older students). Dr. Ed Hallowell has a delightful book for younger children,* A Walk in the Rain With Brain *(2004).*

2. **Help learners attribute their success or lack of it to internal rather than external causes and show them how they have power over the results.**

   "So you think you made a D on your notebook because your teacher doesn't like you and you always get a D no matter what you do? Okay, let's look at that checklist he attached and see if you met all the criteria as stated. If not, let's see what you can do about that for next time."

   "You think you're getting in trouble because the teacher sat you with a bad bunch of kids? Let's brainstorm options for what you can control about the situation and see if we can come up with a reasonable solution for you to try."

   "You think you got first chair in band because you were lucky? Thomas Jefferson said, 'I'm a great believer in luck, and I find the harder I work, the more I have of it.' What do you think he meant by that?"

3. **Treat students' successes as though they are normal, not an isolated example or a fluke.**

   "Yes, Billy, that's it. Now let's go to the next step."
   Not
   "Oh my goodness, you got it RIGHT! Hey everybody, look at this, Billy got the answer right! I can't believe it! Look at me doing my happy dance, Billy! You totally surprised me!"

4. **Help learners seek alternate paths to success when they encounter a roadblock or setback.**

"These timed tests don't seem to be working for you in learning your multiplication facts. Do you have another way you would like to practice them?"

"You appear to be having trouble with the book's explanation of this concept. Let me give you an analogy that might help clarify what it's talking about."

5. **Help students learn the difference between hard work and strategic effort.**

   Often, learners confuse ineffective learning strategies with a lack of ability. Merely telling students to "work hard" is ineffective because expending a lot of misdirected effort toward a goal will not produce the desired results. Careful adult supervision can help students not only to learn efficient study skills, but also to discover the specific strategies that work best for them.

6. **Continually reinforce the idea that the students can work on things within their control, like effort and choices, and they can always control those parts of her life.**

   "It looks like paying attention in class and reviewing your notes each night really worked for you."

   "This makes all of those practice sessions seem worthwhile, doesn't it?"

   "It looks as though you lost points for not fully explaining your answers. What can you do next time to make sure you provide enough evidence to justify your responses?"

7. **Concentrate on improvement rather than on a finite goal. Give continual feedback on progress toward the goal.**

   "You scored 71 out of 100 on this. You have improved 30% over your last attempt. I think your strategy of

(Continued)

(Continued)

slowing down to check for computational errors is really paying off. Do you think you're ready for the next step or do you feel like you need more practice with this one?"

"You remembered to turn in your assignment four times this week without being reminded. That's quite an improvement over last week. How are you motivating yourself to do it on the days you remember? What's different for you on the days you don't remember?"

8. **Keep the learner operating in the zone of proximal development. Tasks that are too easy or too difficult will squash motivation.**

"You've proven you can do the problems in Level 5. Now it's time for you to stretch yourself and move to Level 6. I'm here if you need help on the first few."

"This seems to be overwhelming you a bit. Let's try the same exercise but with fewer terms this time. When you feel confident about the process, we'll move on."

9. **Help students understand that intelligence and talent are not permanent entities. They can be incrementally improved in everyone.**

Chapter 5 explores this more fully.

10. **Use feedback that is specific, constructive, and task specific.**

Observations about student achievement should be statements of fact specifically directed to help the learner improve. More about appropriate feedback is provided in the next section.

Effective Feedback

Adults can foster a healthy attribution view in children with attention to positive modeling and appropriate feedback. An essential point to remember about feedback is exactly that— *feeding back* information to learners will inform them about their progress. It should not judge, label, accuse, excuse, or even praise. The purpose of feedback is to provide instructive knowledge that will enhance the student's performance. A reexamination of the art class scenario will reveal the teacher gave Vincent absolutely nothing that will help him improve as an artist.

Often, adults fail to realize that some of the most effective feedback does not come in the form of statements but rather as questions. Learners appreciate having a fully focused, nonjudgmental adult interested in their work. The art teacher could have asked questions such as "Vincent, how did you know where to put the shadows in your picture?" "Where did you come up with the idea of adding that particular shade of amber?" "How long did you think about what you were going to draw before you began?" "Can you walk me through your thought process?" Students thrive on individual, specific attention from caring adults. It is one of the greatest gifts we can give them.

If the teacher feels she must make a comment, it should be about something Vincent controls. "Vincent, using the bird's-eye perspective was an imaginative way to draw this." Every student who overhears the comment is potentially able to use a novel approach as well; each of them can control that. The teacher is actually setting the stage for students to use more imagination and take greater risks in her classroom. Or the teacher could say, "Vincent, your work shows how much time and effort you put into it." Again, all students in the room have the ability to control their time and effort.

As parents and teachers, we have to get better about helping students realize what they can control and in turn to take responsibility for those very things. Our feedback needs to be honest, specific, nonjudgmental, and given for the express purpose of helping the student get better at something. Here are a few examples.

EFFECTIVE AND INEFFECTIVE PRAISE TO PROMOTE APPROPRIATE ATTRIBUTION

Ineffective: Restricted to global positive reactions. *"Good job!" "Awesome!" "Number One!" "You Rock!"*

Effective: Specifies the particulars of the accomplishment. *"You finished the exercise on time with 90% accuracy." "Your project meets the highest standards on three of the five criteria on the rubric." "You did your assignment every day this week without having to be reminded."*

Ineffective: Shows a bland uniformity that suggests a conditioned response made with minimal attention. *"Oh, that's good." "It's fine." "Uh-huh." "Way to go." "Okay." "Awesome."*

Effective: Show spontaneity, variety, and other signs of credibility that suggest clear attention to the student's accomplishment. *"The details you included in your theme made me feel like I was right there." "The way you played that ball showed some quick thinking." "That example you just gave was one I never would have thought of, and you're exactly right."*

Ineffective: Provides no information at all or gives students information about their status. *"Okay, turn it in." "Yes, I see you're done." "Don't worry, you're fine." "It's acceptable."*

Effective: Provides information to the students about their competence of the value of their accomplishments. *"This paper clearly demonstrates you've attained mastery in this concept. That is something to be proud of!" "In your group today, I noticed it was you who smoothed over the argument and got things back on track." "It seems like you're the one everyone turns to with their computer problems. Thanks for sharing your skills with your classmates."*

Ineffective: Orients students toward comparing themselves with others and thinking about competing. *"Can you make that a little more like Jan's?" "You're never going get into Beta Club with that kind of work." "Well, you're not yet in my top five."*

Effective: Orients students toward better appreciation of their task-related behavior and thinking about problem solving. *"Do you realize you just exceeded your personal best record?" "Show me how you solved that difficult problem." "Let's take a look at the progress you've made these past few days."*

Source: Adapted from Brophy, 1981.

The Littering Experiment

In 1975, R. L. Miller and his associates conducted an experiment on attribution theory and feedback with inner-city fifth graders in Chicago. Their purpose was to test the effectiveness of using attribution theory to change behavior. The problem they addressed was classroom littering. To get a baseline, the researchers visited the classes just before recess and handed out little candies wrapped in plastic. After the children left the room, the researchers counted the number of candy wrappers on the floor and the number in the trashcan. As one might expect with fifth graders, there were many more wrappers on the floor than in the can.

With the control group, nothing was said or done differently during the next two weeks. With the experimental group, however, the following things happened:

- The principal stopped by and commented on how clean the classroom was.
- The janitors left a note on the board saying how easy their classroom was to clean and how neat they were.

- The children made a big poster stating, "We are Anderson's Litter-Conscious Class."
- The principal sent a letter to the class commending them for neatness.
- Their teacher made comments throughout the two-week training period similar to "Neat room, neat kids."

When the researchers returned in two weeks, they again handed out the candies. This time when they counted the wrappers, they found many more in the trashcan than on the floor in the experimental group's room. The control group's room remained basically the same.

The researchers concluded that the students had begun to see themselves as people who don't litter. They believed that their efforts made a difference. The kids realized they had control over their behavior, and they internalized the positive messages from the adults around them. Rather than adhering to the challenge just when the teacher was watching, the students began to see themselves in a new light—as kids who take care of their classroom, and they behaved accordingly.

Later, the researchers added another dimension to the experiment. They took a third group and tried to change their behavior with persuasion. For this group of fifth graders, they structured the following in a two-week period:

- The students got a lesson on ecology.
- The teacher talked about garbage and why it was important to throw it away.
- The teacher read a note from the janitor asking the kids to keep the room cleaner.
- The students were directly told not to throw litter on the floor and given reasons for it.
- The teacher put up a poster that said, "Don't Be A Litterbug!"
- The principal sent a note saying, "Please keep our room clean."

The results were as follows:

Percentage of Paper in Trashcan

	Control	Persuasion	Attribution
Pretest	20%	16%	15%
Posttest	25%	45%	83%
Follow-Up Study	30%	30%	85%

A noteworthy aspect of this study is that the positive behavior of the attribution group not only rose appreciably, but it also actually increased over time. The behavior from the persuasion group rose a little temporarily, but it quickly lost ground. One explanation offered by the researchers is that attribution statements were offered as true statements with no overt signs of coercion. Students weren't asked to do anything new but were given very clear positive attribution messages from the adults around them. The children internalized the positive behavior and changed their self-concepts to match the perception of the adults around them. "The room is neat because we don't litter. We're the kind of people who pick up after ourselves."

On the other hand, the persuasive appeal may have been perceived as a negative attribution in that the children felt targeted as deficient in their habits, which caused a negative reaction to the adults' attempts to change their behavior. How many times have we been told that we "get what we expect" from children? Using the attribution model conveyed a much more powerful message than did the persuasion model because the positive expectation was more genuine.

Rosenthal's Self-Fulfilling Prophecy

In the litter experiment, the children internalized the belief that they were, in fact, neat kids. If you believe you are the kind of person who is neat and does not litter, what happens when you have a candy wrapper in your hand? You throw it in the trashcan. Can adult expectations really have that much influence over children's self-concepts? Most researchers agree that they definitely can and generally do.

Self-fulfilling prophecy, sometimes called the *Pygmalion effect* (which describes the power of expectations), is a concept originally put forth by Robert K. Merton in 1948. It is a theory devised to explain how a belief or an expectation, whether correct or not, affects the outcome of a situation or the way a person (or group) will behave (Rosenthal & Jacobson, 1968). For example, labeling someone as neat may invoke tidy behavior whether that person was already a neat person (Tauber, 1997).

THE KEY PRINCIPLES OF SELF-FULFILLING PROPHECY ARE THE FOLLOWING:

1. We form certain expectations of people or events.

2. We communicate those expectations with various cues.

3. People tend to respond to these cues by adjusting their behavior to match them.

4. The result is that the original expectation becomes true.

Most parents and teachers have witnessed countless incidents where we "got what we expected" in children. That can be a positive or a negative thing. I have a stepson, Andy, who in elementary school was thought to have low-functioning academic ability and was labeled a slow learner. The adults in his life expected little of him, and he lived right *down* to their expectations. In middle school, when it was discovered that he had an IQ well above average and that most of his struggles with learning were caused by processing problems, such as dyslexia, his teachers treated him in a totally different way. The adults around him began to expect much more of him, and they would not tolerate his learned helplessness. At that point, his life turned around, and his grades, performance, and self-concept improved remarkably. This young man who was told in the second grade that he would probably never graduate from high school now has two master's degrees and is a successful practicing family therapist.

The power of expectation apparently even carries over to rodents. In 1963, researcher Robert Rosenthal, a professor of sociology at Harvard, performed an experiment in which he told a group of graduate students that he had developed a strain of supersmart rats that could run mazes quickly. He then passed out perfectly normal rats at random, telling half of the students they had the new "bright" rats and the other half that they got "dull" rats. The rats that were believed to be bright improved daily in running the maze ran faster and more accurately. The rats that were believed to be dull suffered all kinds of problems, such as refusing to run the maze, not running fast, and not running accurately. Their trainers' expectations seemed to have influenced the efficiency of the rats' performance (Rosenthal & Fode, 1963). When I tell that story to teachers, I always ask them to consider if a trainer's expectation can have that much influence on a rat, can we dare ignore teacher expectations of students?

Wanting to apply his theory to actual children, Rosenthal and Lenore Jacobson (1968) worked with elementary school children from 18 classrooms. They randomly chose 20% of the children from each room and told the teachers they were "intellectual bloomers." They explained that these children could be expected to show remarkable gains during the year. The experimental children showed average IQ gains of two points in verbal ability, seven points in reasoning and four points in overall IQ. The intellectual bloomers really did bloom!

Many studies have since replicated Rosenthal and Jacobson's original study, and their original hypothesis has been validated. Teacher expectation does affect student performance. After three decades of research, Rosenthal and Jacobson (1992) have determined four factors they feel explain the results of these experiments:

1. The *emotional climate* was affected by expectations. (Teachers acted warmer toward students they expected to do well.)

2. The *behaviors* of teachers were different. (Teachers gave the perceived bloomers more difficult material to study.)

3. The *opportunities to speak out in class* were different. (Teachers gave the perceived bloomers more opportunities to respond in class and more time to answer questions.)

4. The *level of detailed feedback* about performance was different. (Teachers gave the perceived bloomers more informative feedback.) (Adapted from Rosenthal, 1994)

Three of the factors cited by Rosenthal support principles already presented in this book. Factor 2, the teachers gave the perceived bloomers more difficult material to study, validates the zone of proximal development theory. Students who were asked to stretch their abilities were more successful.

Factor 3, the perceived bloomers were given more opportunities to speak out and more time to answer questions, reiterates the importance of scaffolding. Part of giving students a reasonable chance at success is granting them the opportunities they need and allowing them the time they require to be successful in their responses.

Factor 4, teachers gave the perceiver bloomers more informative feedback, addresses concepts presented in this chapter as well as in Chapter 5. Successful student growth is enhanced by knowledgeable feedback from responsive adults.

Adult expectations do, in fact, greatly impact self-concept in young people. One might ask, if expectation is that important in helping a child develop a positive self-image, then why was the teacher's feedback to Vincent inappropriate? She obviously expects him to be the best artist, so why would her words be counterproductive to that end? Aren't we just splitting hairs here about word choice?

Communicating high expectations is a tricky business. The subtleties of our words are not lost on students, and they carry very strong messages. While it is indeed desirable to let students know we believe in them and their abilities, it is equally important that we direct their attention to attributes that help them build a sense of self-efficacy—their choices and their efforts. The power of our words and the nuances of our messages are further explored in Chapter 5.

Mindset

The Key to Self-Motivation

· ·
You have a choice. Mindsets are just beliefs.
They're powerful beliefs, but they're just something
in your mind, and you can change your mind.
— Carol Dweck, 2006
· ·

Chapter 4 begins with a scenario about a teacher praising her student's artwork. When discussing the art-class scenario, audience participants are usually quick to point out the teacher is labeling Vincent and is virtually setting him up for failure by calling him the class artist. I agree the praise is potentially very destructive for Vincent but probably not for the reason they are thinking—(i.e., that Vincent is going to get clobbered on the playground at lunch for making everyone else look bad). There is something else going on that is so subtle and so pervasive in our culture that most people don't think twice about it. Chapter 5 examines an extension of attribution theory and self-regulation. Dr. Carol Dweck's *mindset* theory has profound implications and insights for the concept of fall down seven times, get up eight.

In a poll conducted in the mid-1990s, 85% of parents believed that praising children's ability or intelligence when they perform well makes them feel smart (Mueller & Dweck, 1996). Recent research by Dr. Carol Dweck and associates proves that praising aptitude or mental power has the unintentional effect of making children feel fragile, vulnerable, and less likely to try new things.

Dr. Dweck, a leader in the fields of motivation, personality, and developmental psychology, has studied attribution theory and its attending implications for the human psyche for more than 30 years. Through rigorous research studies, she has taken attribution theory and self-regulation to the next logical step, an area she calls *mindset*.

Let's begin with a little test from Dweck's 2006 *Mindset: The New Psychology of Success.* Here is the scenario:

ELIZABETH'S DILEMMA

Nine-year-old Elizabeth was on her way to her first gymnastics meet. Lanky, flexible, and energetic, she was just right for gymnastics and she loved it. Of course, she was a little nervous about competing, but she was good at gymnastics and felt confident of doing well. She had even thought about the perfect place in her room to hang the ribbons she would win.

In the first event, the floor exercises, Elizabeth went first. Although she did a nice job, the scoring changed after the first few girls and she lost. Elizabeth also did well in the other events, but not well enough to win. By the end of the evening, she had received no ribbons and was devastated.

What would you do if you were Elizabeth's parents, teacher, or coach?

1. Tell Elizabeth *you* thought she was the best.

2. Tell her she was robbed of a ribbon that was rightfully hers.

> 3. Reassure her that gymnastics is not that impor-
>   tant.
>
> 4. Tell her she has the ability and will surely win
>   the next time.
>
> 5. Tell her she didn't deserve to win. (pp. 174–175)

Really think about which answer you would choose as Elizabeth's adult advocate. You can be her parent, her teacher, her coach, or another influential role model. You probably don't like any of the options entirely, but this is a forced choice, so pick one. Don't look ahead for the correct answer. Don't try to combine answers or hedge your bets. Really be honest with yourself and pick which of the five choices you would most likely make.

Here's what Dweck (2006) says about the five possible reactions. If you chose the first one (*you* thought she was the best), you are being disingenuous. You were at the meet and you witnessed the other girls outperforming Elizabeth after she did her routine. She knows you saw the same thing she did. To deny that it happened or to say that you still think she should have won is simply not true. She will either think that you have impaired judgment or you are just telling her what she wants to hear. Neither of those is going to help her in the end. You have given her no helpful information to improve her performance, and she is left with the sense that she cannot rely on your evaluation.

If you picked the second choice (that she was denied a ribbon that was rightfully hers), you are basically instructing her to look for external reasons when she fails. Ironically, I have had parents in workshops who choose this option because they think it helps their children understand that sometimes the system works against them, and they should learn not to take it personally. While I agree that at certain times most of us have questioned the decisions of judges, referees, and the like,

I never want to teach young learners that no matter how hard they work, how valiant their efforts, or how big of a risk they take, they really are just victims of arbitrary whims of others. As we discussed in Chapter 4, it is critical that students concentrate on those things they *can* control.

The third choice (reassure her that gymnastics is not that important) devalues her passion and also tells her that she should give up if she is not immediately successful. As in the first and second options, she is given no useful information to improve her performance. And with this option she is more or less encouraged to quit.

The fourth choice (she has the ability and will surely win the next one) is overwhelmingly the most popular choice among audience participants. Most admit they are a little leery of the last part of the choice, "and will surely win the next one," because no one can accurately predict that, but they like the idea of praising Elizabeth's ability. Dweck (2006) says this fourth choice is probably the worst and most dangerous one of all. She believes this inappropriate praise leads to a sense of entitlement and diminishes effort. The rest of this chapter will further illuminate the counterproductively of such a statement.

In my experience, the least-chosen option is the last one. If you chose the fifth option, you agree with Dweck's researchers. No one would suggest that you say something horrid like "Oh Elizabeth, you were awful! You deserved to lose. You embarrassed yourself as well as our entire family." However, effective coaches everywhere tell us that this is the time to be perfectly candid with her: "Elizabeth, I know you are disappointed. No one likes to lose, but truly you haven't yet earned a ribbon. Let's review the events of today and see if we can figure out where you need to improve. If this is something you really want, then you're going to have to work for it. Let's make a plan for what you are going to do to get better for next time." The parent or teacher here needs to give Elizabeth the information about how to improve her performance. Honest, detailed, nonjudgmental feedback will be more likely to inspire her to strive to meet high standards.

Once I explain Dweck's (2006) reasoning, most adults agree the fifth choice is the preferred one, but why do so few of them choose it to begin with? I think it is because in much of our culture overpraising children has become the norm. We are so afraid of hurting their self-esteem that we exaggerate their accomplishments, overrate their abilities, and sugarcoat any kind of criticism. We try to protect our children from failure by clearing obstacles from their paths rather than by teaching them how to deal forthrightly with stumbling blocks. We try to hide their deficits rather than help them develop purposeful steps to correct them. It has become common practice in our society to praise students for their success on easy tasks or when they do things quickly and perfectly. What then is the implication when the task is not easy or when they make mistakes? Does that mean they are no longer smart or talented or praiseworthy? It is my belief that many adults unknowingly send damaging messages to our children under the guise of praise.

Fixed Mindset/Growth Mindset

Through a myriad of research studies with learners from age three through university students, Dweck (2000) and her associates have determined that humans have belief systems that act concurrently with attribution theory. She proposes that people basically have two ways of viewing their circumstances, with either *fixed mindset* or *growth mindset.* Her studies have led her to conclude that mindset drives every aspect of our lives and holds the key for self-motivation and self-efficacy.

Fixed Mindset (entity theory) is based on the idea that there is a predetermined amount of gifts, talent, skills, intelligence, and the like in each human being. People who have this belief system think that ability and talent are finite entities and are *fixed* from birth. This conviction leads them to a constant struggle to maintain their appearance of looking smart rather than seeking challenges, which may, however temporarily, make them look as if they are not so smart (or talented or gifted). They live in fear of being measured by failure, which they believe may label them in a permanent way. People with a fixed mindset are consumed with proving themselves repeatedly because their self-worth is derived from the appearance of having intelligence and/or abilities. They see setbacks and mistakes as threats to their ego and usually lose confidence and motivation when work is no longer easy for them. Not matter how smart or talented they are, they often lose their coping mechanisms in the face of setbacks.

Many children who sail through elementary school are told how smart they are because they don't have to work hard. They are praised for being superior to their peers, and they believe that effort is for those who are not smart. Rosenthal's (1968) self-fulfilling prophecy works for them temporarily because the adults in their lives expect them to be the best, and they can easily accommodate the confidence of the people most important to them for a while. However, problems start to emerge when they begin to face even normal setbacks and failure. The fixed-mindset person needs a steady diet of success.

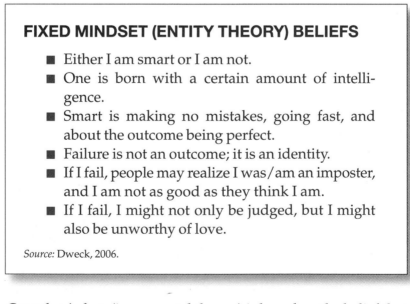

FIXED MINDSET (ENTITY THEORY) BELIEFS

- Either I am smart or I am not.
- One is born with a certain amount of intelligence.
- Smart is making no mistakes, going fast, and about the outcome being perfect.
- Failure is not an outcome; it is an identity.
- If I fail, people may realize I was/am an imposter, and I am not as good as they think I am.
- If I fail, I might not only be judged, but I might also be unworthy of love.

Source: Dweck, 2006.

Growth mindset (incremental theory) is based on the belief that whatever intelligence and abilities a person has, he can always cultivate more through focused effort. People with growth mindset believe that virtually all people can get better at anything if they try. As Dweck points out,

> It's not that people holding this theory deny that there are differences among people in how much they know or in how quickly they master certain things at present. It's just that they focus on the idea that everyone, with effort and guidance, can increase their intellectual abilities. (Mueller & Dweck quoted in Dweck, 2000, p. 3)

Learners who have a growth mindset believe intelligence is malleable and can be developed through education and hard work. Their focus is on learning and improving rather than on maintaining an appearance. Growth mindset learners understand that just because some people can do things easily with little or no training doesn't mean others can't do it (and sometimes even better) with training, work, and perseverance (Dweck, 2006). Students with growth mindset are energized by challenge and see setbacks and failures as temporary and mainly attributable to lack of effort or focus rather than a deficiency of ability or intelligence. They see mistakes as problems to be solved. These learners will often forgo the chance to look smart to learn something new.

GROWTH MINDSET (INCREMENTAL THEORY) BELIEFS

- A belief that effort is a positive, constructive force.
- Development and progress are important—not just the product or achievement.
- One can substantially change, stretch, and grow, and that is desirable.
- Brains can become *bigger.* Challenge is good.
- Being on a learning edge is the smart thing to do.

Source: Dweck, 2006.

Differences in Fixed Mindset and Growth Mindset

Dweck (2006) points out that as long as students have success in their endeavors there is little difference between those with fixed mindset and those with growth mindset. Confidence levels and self-esteem are not necessarily related to mindset. The divergent patterns usually emerge when the learner begins to address more difficult work. Because the fixed mindset learner has a strong desire to look smart, he has a tendency to avoid challenges, give up easily when confronted with obstacles, see effort as fruitless or demeaning, ignore useful criticism, and feel threatened by the success of others. As a result, this learner may plateau early and achieve less than his full potential.

Since the growth mindset learner has a strong desire to learn, she has a tendency to embrace challenges, persist in the face of setbacks, see effort as a logical step toward mastery, learn from criticism, and find lessons and inspiration in the success of others. As a result, this learner will reach ever-higher levels of achievement.

It is revealing to examine the statements about feeling smart from both the fixed mindset students and the growth mindset students:

WHEN DO YOU FEEL SMART?

Fixed Mindset

- "It's when I don't make any mistakes."
- "When I finish something fast and it's perfect."
- "When something is easy for me, but other people can't do it."

It's about being perfect right now.

Growth Mindset

- "When it's really hard, and I try really hard, and I can do something I couldn't do before"

■ "When I work on something a long time and start to figure it out."

For them, it's not about immediate perfection. It's about learning something over time: confronting a challenge and making progress.

Source: Dweck, 2006.

Students, Puzzles, and Mindsets

Dweck's (1999) team did an experiment to determine if they could influence children's mindsets. They gave children puzzles to work on and then provided one line of praise. They either said, "You did really well; you must be very smart" (reinforcing fixed mindset), or they said, "You did really well; you must have worked really hard" (reinforcing growth mindset). The puzzles got progressively harder.

When challenged by puzzles they could not solve, students with a fixed mindset made comments such as "I'm not very good at these kinds of things" and "I don't like these puzzles anymore." But students with a growth mindset said things such as "I need to take a little more time with this," or "This is fun."

At the conclusion of the session, researchers offered the children either a harder puzzle that they could learn from or one that was the same as the one they completed successfully. The majority of the kids praised for their intelligence wanted the easier puzzle—it was more important to them to maintain the illusion of being smart than to pursue something new and challenging. On the other hand, more than 90% of students praised for effort chose a harder puzzle. Why? Dweck explains that "When we praise children for the effort and hard work that leads to achievement, they want to keep engaging in that process. They are not diverted from the task of learning by a concern with how smart they might—or might not—look" (1999, p. 2).

In study after study, the researchers found that inappropriate praise does more harm than good. When adults praise children for their ability or intelligence, they are helping create a fixed mindset for the child. Feedback on effort, perseverance, and ingenuity help create a growth mindset in the child.

It is mind boggling to think that all the unrestricted praise we have heaped on kids since the 1970s has actually done more harm than good. But what behavioral psychologists now tell us is that inappropriate praise generally has the opposite effect of empowering learners. Praise for tasks that are too simple in the first place signals learners that we don't think they are capable of more challenging work. Praise for intelligence or talent can create a situation where students become more concerned about the label than the learning. Both positive and negative labels can have devastating effects on students.

One of the hardest things I have had to do in my work with student motivation is to stop myself from praising children's innate abilities or intelligence. For so long, I have told them things like "You are so smart." "You are such a great singer." "You are going to rule the world." I am still working on changing my feedback to statements like "Wow, you stuck with that until you solved it." "I can tell how hard you practiced that vocal arrangement." "You showed a lot of courage with the stand you took on that issue." My head knows what is the right thing to say, but habit keeps me wanting to pump out the old labels.

Taking the Joy From the Artist

When the teacher in Chapter 4 praises Vincent on his art ability, she is reinforcing a fixed mindset mentality. Vincent may come to view his status as the class artist as more important than anything he can learn from pursuing different techniques or exploring other avenues of presentation with his art. He now has the pressure of always being the best at whatever he does in art class, and that can potentially erode his love for art and his confidence in doing it. Labeling children has many unforeseen consequences.

How many times in a family is one child the designated responsible one, another is the entertainer of the family, and still another is the child destined for med school. These labels create conflict among the siblings. ("Well, look what Mr. Responsible just pulled." "She's not the only one in this family who can be funny." "Oh, like I'm not smart enough to go to med school even if I wanted to.") They also limit the ways the labeled child sees himself.

Labels can set up unrealistic expectations and make a child even more vulnerable to feelings of inadequacy. In my family, my oldest brother was labeled the smart one. I was labeled the writer, and my youngest of three brothers was labeled the charmer. My other brother (third in line), whose surprise arrival came 17 months after I was born, had trouble establishing his particular calling. As a child, he just never excelled at anything in particular. In his middle school years, he was very interested in art. He dabbled with painting, drawing, chalks, and other media. He truly enjoyed what he was doing.

My parents seized the opportunity finally to give him a label. He was to be our family artist. They poured all kinds of praise and support to their exceptional son and went on and on about how talented he was. Of course, they did this with the utmost confidence they were doing the right thing. Surely, a child showered with compliments and predictions of future success would thrive in his endeavors. Not so.

In high school, the family artist took an advanced class with an array of other students interested in art. Some were far more experienced than he; some produced works superior to his, and soon my brother began to feel inadequate and intimidated. Not wanting to lose the approval of my parents, he began to hedge on some of his assignments. Rather than draw and paint original work, he began to copy, and even trace, some of his pictures. I remember my mother being horrified to learn that one of his paintings she had abundantly praised was actually something he had "borrowed" from another source.

And why was she surprised? After basically being told that his claim to fame in our family was that he was a gifted artist, how could this young boy possibly take the risk of letting down the people he cared about? Once he was identified as the artist, he did everything he could to maintain that identity—even cheat. The label robbed him of his joy in visual imagery, the thrill of learning new things, and the excitement of taking chances—even if it meant he would only temporarily stumble. He was far more concerned about appearing to be a talented artist than in actually becoming one. It was a very sad time in his life.

A footnote to this story is that same brother worked in the airline industry, created a themed restaurant, learned to sing and play the guitar, studied handwriting analysis, became an amateur magician, and wrote two novels (not published) before taking his life in 1992. I always felt that each endeavor he pursued was more for the sake of proving himself to others than for enjoying the journey or even the achievement. He was a very talented, intelligent, and personable guy, but he never really learned how to deal with setbacks or recover from failure. His fixed mindset kept him from seeing in himself what everyone else saw in him—a great person with the ability to do virtually anything he wanted if he had stuck with it and put his heart and soul into it.

Gifted Kids and Coping With Failure

If you ask most people which students are most likely to cheat, you will usually get the answer, "The least prepared." That is not the case. According to Dweck (2006), the students most likely to cheat are students who have been labeled *gifted*. If you think about it, it makes sense; those are the students with the most to lose. They are the ones whose identity is caught up with an appearance of being the smartest, the brightest, and the best.

Gifted kids are told in countless ways how special they are, how superior they are, and/or how much is expected of them. The pressure to produce is relentless. So often, these kids are simply unable to relax and enjoy the process of learning.

As a science teacher, one of my favorite teaching strategies was to begin my first day of class with some kind of discrepant event. Piaget (1974) makes the case that students never really open their minds to new learning until the old learning is somehow shaken to create a disequilibrium (cognitive dissonance). He maintains that teachers who begin by stating facts and layering new knowledge on top of old knowledge encourage students to be lazy and unmotivated. So rather than stating the definitions of "observations" and "inferences," I set up a little demonstration at the beginning of class. I asked students to forget all their prior knowledge of an everyday phenomenon I was about to demonstrate. I told them I merely wanted their observations (what can be known from the five senses) and nothing else. I emphasized how important it was they only use their powers of observation.

I uncovered a candle sitting on my lab table. I struck a match, lit the wick, and allowed the candle to burn for a couple of minutes. I blew out the candle and asked students to quickly write their observations. Most students wrote they saw a flickering flame, they saw smoke when I blew out the candle, and they smelled something burning. A few wrote that they saw what appeared to be liquid sliding down the candle.

In our discussion of the event, however, there were usually a couple of students whose identity was wrapped up in feeling intellectually superior. To set themselves apart from the crowd they would throw in comments such as "Well, the reason the wax is melting is that the heat of the flame caused the molecules to move faster and change the state of matter from a solid to a liquid." "The reason the wick burned and the candle melted is because the wick is made of string, which is highly flammable, and the candle is made of wax, which is not highly flammable." Those comments usually shut down conversation from other students, who became intimidated by their more verbose peers.

I thanked all the students who had contributed their ideas. I then began to explain in science class we needed to be open to many ideas and should be on the lookout for new discoveries because they would find over and over again in this class, all in this world is not as it appears to be. As I admonished them to be open to new vistas and not try always to give me an answer I wanted to hear, I began eating the candle—wick and all. I explained that the observations that were made (seeing the flame, smelling a burn, seeing the smoke) were quite accurate, but the other comments were not observations at all. They were inferences based on prior experience. Thus, the students who make only observations were correct, and those who used their prior knowledge, in this instance, were incorrect.

Their mouths were agape. Most of them hooted with laughter and demanded to know "What was that really?" I explained it was a candle, but not a traditional one, and I asked them to write some possible explanations for homework. In actuality, the candle demonstration is a classic science teacher demo. I had cut a raw potato in the shape of a candle and put it in a glass candleholder. The wick was a raw almond sliver I had slightly burned the night before to give it the appearance of a string wick. Most students figured out I had made the candle out of some kind of food, but few guessed that the wick was not string.

As we discussed, the demo the next day I reiterated the importance of knowing the difference between "observations" and "inferences." Most students were enthusiastically engaged and enjoyed having been duped. However, invariably I had at least one student who sulked, pouted, and/or outwardly objected to the demo. As one identified gifted/talented (G/T) student told me, "I don't think it's fair to lie to students." In other words, because this student had initially gleefully put other students in their places by elaborating on the cohesiveness of molecules only to be proved absolutely wrong in this case, he felt defensive and even angry. It was more important for him to look smart than to learn something new.

Gifted Kids and Fixed Mindsets

Teachers of G/T frequently tell me about asking their students to try something innovative or novel and having them react quite negatively. If the students can't master the concept immediately or demonstrate superiority right away, some don't want to try. For them, it is about being perfect right now and being recognized for it. They fear if they falter or take too much time, others will not perceive them as the smartest and brightest.

Parents relate that often their G/T children's default reaction to new concepts or experiences is "This is stupid, and I don't want to do it." Having had two boys in our house who were labeled, G/T, I can certainly attest to that situation. My oldest son, Maverick, was accepted into the new G/T program at our elementary school when he was in the fourth grade. As a parent, I felt proud that my firstborn was selected. I assumed that his new program would stimulate all kinds of knowledge seeking and advanced skill acquisition. I'm not sure that's what happened. I think what he mostly got from the program was a sense of entitlement that basically told him he was smarter than everyone else. Occasionally, I overheard some of the kids in his gifted class make disparaging remarks about their peers who were "not so bright." I think designers of G/T programs need to be heedful of mindsets and be cautious about encouraging growth rather than fixed mindsets in learners. I don't think Maverick was able to enjoy the process of learning like most kids because he constantly felt he had to live up to the expectations about him always being the best—at everything. He mostly liked games he could repeatedly win, and he quickly lost interest in areas where he was not immediately superior.

Some of his teachers singled him out with comments like "How could you not make an A on that assignment? I thought you were supposed to be gifted." While many people use the label G/T to describe a student's superior aptitude in all areas of learning, it is important to remember that no student is gifted in everything. The method for selecting G/T students varies widely among school systems. Some include the creative arts, and some do not. Some are heavily weighted toward students with superior reading ability and others not so much. In my experience, I have never met a student who was gifted in every aspect of school or in every one of Howard Garner's (1993) identified intelligences. And once the student is labeled as gifted, there is often an added pressure to be superior in every aspect of life.

Putting G/T students with a growth mindset together can inspire them to new heights. However, for students with a fixed mindset, being relegated to a group of similar cohorts, can be quite overwhelming. For many of them, it is the first time they have competed with peers of equal or even superior intellect and/or talent, and they begin to doubt their ability.

A young man I know quite well is an extraordinary learner. In the small town where he lived, he was seldom challenged by his high school curriculum. He studied very little but was able to finesse good grades through his charisma, resourcefulness, and innate intelligence. He applied for and was accepted to the Louisiana School for Math, Science, and the Arts (LSMSA, an elite school for the gifted and talented) when he was 16 years old. He was thrilled to go to a residential school on a college campus in a town far from where his parents lived. He arrived on campus full of anticipation and eager to be challenged by teachers of the highest caliber. There was one problem. The former top-of-the-class kid was now just one among dozens who had also been the top-of-the-class in their worlds prior to arriving at LSMSA. He was challenged in ways he had never been before not only by his teachers but also by his peers. He was among a group of highly competitive, high-performing, seemingly self-confident students selected from all over the state. There were a number of difficulties going on in his personal life at that time, but not the least of them was his belief that maybe he was not supposed to be there. He was overwhelmed by the exhaustive demands of the faculty and the seemingly endless endurance of the other students. For the first time in his life, he had to ask himself, "Am I as smart as I thought I was? Was it all a myth? Do I really belong here?" By the end of that first year, he was gone. He left the program. He did not graduate from high school. He eventually received a general equivalency diploma (GED) and went on with his life, but the setback in high school really unsettled him. With his fixed mindset, he believed that if you fail—if you are not the best—it has all been a waste of time. He saw no value in the learning he got from the experience (as would someone with a growth mindset).

This young man was basically hamstrung by unrealized potential. What a horrible curse to put on a person. Here is a young man who has been told all of his life, "You are the best. You are the smartest. You are better than your peers. You don't have to study or work hard because you have natural ability, and that ability will take you wherever you want to go." We have been telling kids that for years, but it's simply not true. No one achieves anything of value without hard work and effort. The belief that hard work and effort are for those who are not gifted undermines the very success of those who so doggedly crave it.

Fostering a Growth Mindset in Children

In addition to ceasing to praise learners for their abilities or intelligence, adults can foster a growth mindset in children with appropriate feedback that focuses on how they can improve. We live in a society fixated on instant success, effortless performance, and natural talent. Adults must help students understand that virtually every successful athlete, entertainer, and scholar got where they are through deliberate practice and focused effort. We can tell them stories about successful people that emphasize hard work and love of learning. We can teach them about how the brain works and how it is possible to grow smarter. And most important, we can model a growth mindset attitude.

Dr. Dweck offers a twist on a rather common event. I was reading an anecdote she wrote about a child coming home from primary school full of excitement to tell his mom that he was the first one through with the assignment and that he didn't even have to try because it was so easy for him. Immediately I began to ponder things I would probably have said to my child such as "That's amazing, honey. You are so smart. You really take after my side of the family." But Dweck points out that probably the best response from the parent would be something like "Well, that's not fair. You didn't get a chance to learn anything today. Let's go talk to that teacher and see if we can't get her to give you an assignment that will help you learn something new."

When I tell audiences that story, they always laugh at the irony of what Dweck suggests the parent should say. But let's think about it. Isn't that the exact right response? When we praise children for doing what is easily mastered, aren't we essentially telling them we are more appreciative of appearances than of real achievement? Don't we really want learners who constantly push their boundaries and diligently strive to attain more through their efforts?

Children are so eager for adult attention. It is such a simple thing to look them in the eyes and genuinely listen to what they are telling us—or to ask them questions to have them extend their thinking. From my experience as a teacher and a mother, I can tell you that kids have limitless means for getting adults to pay attention to them. Unfortunately, many adults believe that paying attention means praising a child's every move. Research has taught us that what children are starved for is feedback. It doesn't have to be effusive, over-the-top praise. It just needs to be honest, specific, and helpful. Feedback is not about labeling or praising or scolding. It is about giving learners information that will help them make improvements.

Feedback That Changes Perspectives

A word of caution about effective feedback is in order here. As previously mentioned, telling children they simply need to work *harder* is not sufficient feedback. It is important to remember that inefficient learners often have no idea what the adults mean by that statement. I've watched students stare at a single page in a textbook for extended periods who believe they studied hard. Rather than just admonishing students to work hard at something, we need to model the effective preparation we want them to use. Whether we are talking about a study skill, an athletic performance, or some other area we need to guide students in specific techniques for practicing effectively and efficiently.

Finishing the discussion about the artwork scenario (Chapter 4), I usually ask participants what they thought was the worst thing the teacher said to Vincent. I get all kinds of responses but seldom the one I seeking. From my standpoint, I think the worst thing she said was, *"You know I never could draw. I'm a horrible artist! From now on, when I need something illustrated on the board, would you do it for me?"* Not only does she model a fixed mindset, what is her solution to her belief that she cannot draw? She gives a perfect example of learned helplessness (i.e., "It's too hard for me, so you'll have to do it for me."). What kind of role modeling is that? She missed a perfect opportunity to say, "I've always wanted to improve my drawing ability. Vincent, you have inspired me to check out some library books on the subject and start practicing." Or "Vincent, I would love to learn how to add dimension like you did, will you show me how to do that?"

As adults, we need to talk more about our struggles and how we cope with setbacks. Dweck (2008) suggests that parents and teachers help children enjoy the process of learning by expressing positive views of effort, challenges, and mistakes.

- "Boy, this is hard—this is fun."
- "Oh, sorry, that was too easy—no fun! Let's so something more challenging that you can learn from."
- "Let's talk about what we struggled with today and learned from. I'll go first."
- "Mistakes are so interesting. Here's a wonderful mistake. Let's see what we can learn from it." (Dweck, 2008, p. 40)

Conclusion

Dr. Dweck acknowledges that people can have different mindsets about diverse areas of their lives. A person can have a growth mindset about her intelligence and a fixed mindset about her athletic ability or any number of combinations about aspects of her life dealing with artistic ability, business sense, self-discipline, and the like. And as Dweck has proven, mindsets can be changed. She and her team have written curriculum for that purpose: *Brainology.* In it, students are taught specific lessons about how people can literally grow more intelligent and how anyone can get better at anything by working smarter.

I think Carol Dweck's greatest contribution to the study of student motivation is providing parents and teachers with powerful research about how to help students become their own best advocates. We can empower rather than entitle learners by teaching them to focus on things they can control—their effort, their perseverance, their attitudes, and their commitment. We can teach them that failure is not permanent and that it does not define you—rather it is an important step to falling down seven times, getting up eight.

> *The paradox of excellence is that it is built upon the foundations of failure.*
>
> —Matthew Syed, 2010

What Do I Get for Doing It?

(Examining Rewards)

. . . .

The reward of a thing well done is having done it.
—Ralph Waldo Emerson

. . . .

THE OLD MAN AND THE TRASH CAN DILEMMA

(ADAPTED FROM AN OLD JEWISH FOLKTALE)

A wise old gentleman retired and purchased a modest home near a junior high school. He spent the first few weeks of his retirement in peace and contentment. Then a new school year began. The next afternoon, three young boys, full of youthful, afterschool enthusiasm, came down his street, beating merrily on every trashcan they encountered. The crashing percussion continued day after day until finally the wise old man decided it was time to take action.

(Continued)

(Continued)

The next afternoon, he walked out to meet the young percussionists as they banged their way down the street. Stopping them, he said, "You kids are a lot of fun. I like to see you express your exuberance like that. In fact, I used to do the same thing when I was your age. Will you do me a favor? I'll give you each a dollar if you'll promise to come around every day and do your thing." The kids were elated and continued to do a bang-up job on the trashcans.

After a few days, the old-timer greeted the kids again, but this time he had a sad smile on his face. "This recession's really putting a big dent in my income," he told them. "From now on, I'll only be able to pay you 50 cents to beat on the cans."

The noisemakers were obviously displeased, but they did accept his offer and continued their afternoon ruckus. A few days later, the wily retiree approached them again as they drummed their way down the street.

"Look," he said, "I haven't received my Social Security check yet, so I'm not going to be able to give you more than 25 cents. Will that be okay?"

"A lousy quarter!" the drum leader exclaimed. "If you think we're going to waste our time, beating these cans around for a quarter, you're nuts! No way, mister. We quit!" And the old man enjoyed peace.

This story is a favorite of mine for demonstrating that rewards can be a double-edged sword. It is impossible to discuss the topic of self-motivation without considering the effects of rewards. We need to ask ourselves many questions: Do rewards move students toward a growth mindset? Do they build resilience and self-efficacy in students? Chapter 6 explores the relationship between *extrinsic rewards* and empowering students to lead successful lives.

Rewards are used copiously in numerous schools and households by adults convinced they work. A number of researchers raise strong objections to extrinsic rewards because they believe they subvert self-motivation in learners. Frustrated adults often ask why the most common question they hear from young people asked to do even ordinary tasks is, "What do I *get* for doing it?"

Probably the short answer to the question of why learners respond that way is that we have taught our children very potent lessons about rewards we never intended. Some of us believed that by offering compensation, prizes, and other external tokens of gratitude, we were inspiring children to do things they normally would not do on their own. We inundated them with praise, cheerleading, and rewards of every type. I remember thinking what a great teacher I was because I gave kids so many treats, prizes, recognitions, and bonuses with the well-intended purpose of motivating them to do things that were "in their best interest" but not always that enticing. My thought was that when students recognized the positive effects of things like doing homework, showing good citizenship, and other desirable actions, they would internalize the behaviors long term. Where did I get that idea in the first place?

My Parents and Rewards

It wasn't from my parents. Both of them grew up during the Great Depression. Both were brought up under austere conditions and were told they were lucky to have a roof over their heads and enough food to eat. They worked hard, complained little, and were generally grateful for what they had. They worked diligently at school so they could get ahead. They worked conscientiously at home to help their families (my dad was the ninth of ten children). And both my parents had additional jobs outside their homes to help supplement the meager subsistence their families had. They "grew up hard," so to speak.

Consequently, my parents' views on child rearing were more lenient than those of my grandparents. But while they wanted their children to live a more comfortable life without the day-to-day struggle for survival, they definitely believed children should behave appropriately because it was the right thing to do. Gifts were for Christmas and birthdays and not for other times no matter how well we behaved. My three brothers and I were punished if we broke rules or if we performed poorly in school. Rebukes were swift and severe if we disappointed our parents. And any complaint of "I'm bored" or "I don't feel like doing that" met with immediate assignment of additional chores or consequences. I think the generation of parents in the 1950s and early 1960s generally shared a core belief that doing well in school was the student's job. If there was a problem at school, my parents blamed us. My mother and father believed that children should be subservient to their elders.

My Love Affair With Rewards

Then along came my generation. We began having children in the early 1970s. We were barraged with psychological advice admonishing us to put our children's interests first. Most of us felt that our parents had been too strict, too critical, and too demanding. Noted pediatrician Benjamin Spock (1973) told us that parents need to be much less rigid and far more permissive in rearing children. Canter and Canter (1976) told us it was far preferable to catch kids being good and reward them than constantly to point out their mistakes and/or punish them. It all made sense. After all, even my grandmother used to say, "You catch more flies with honey than with vinegar."

And so it began. We focused on building up our children with much praise, encouragement, and extrinsic rewards as a way of thanking them for making appropriate decisions. When we sometimes felt angry toward our ungrateful youngsters, we turned those negative feelings inward—to guilt. Often to assuage our guilt, we gave them more praise and more rewards to prove the love we truly felt for them. It was all well meant, and we acted in the good faith that we were far superior parents to our children than those who had gone before us. We failed to realize there is a long-term cost to all the rewards and praise we showered on our offspring.

There is abundant research linking the inappropriate use of rewards to the loss of motivation, but I didn't find that out until later. My first inkling that all was not well with rewards came from personal observations. In my middle school classroom, I made a practice of awarding appropriate behavior with Super Citizen Awards. Each award had a tear-off coupon at the bottom to be used as a raffle entry for a large prize that I awarded each Friday. The only way a student was eligible for the big prize was to accumulate Super Citizen Awards. I kept a record of my recipients to ensure I doled them out equitably and that no one was left out for too long. Soon students would wait to see me coming and then jump to help a friend retrieve a fallen book or hold the door open for another person. If I didn't immediately say, "Oh, that's worth an award," they would call attention to the act. Sometimes students would complain and say, "Oh, I've been being so good and I haven't gotten a certificate in a long time." I would reply that Super Citizen Award rules did not allow them to ask me for an award; I had to "catch them" being good. I would smile and tell them, "Don't worry, if you continue using appropriate behavior I will eventually notice it and give you an award. Keep up the good work!" I thought my plan was going swimmingly.

My Aha Moment With Rewards

Then a fellow teacher friend and I went to a training session sponsored by a professional education group. We had no idea what the three-day conference was about, but we were excited we had been invited to be trained as "emerging leaders." When we arrived, we stood side by side to sign in. My greeter took my name and basic information and welcomed me to the conference. My friend, Joyce, had a similar greeter only hers handed her a little piece of laminated paper and said, "Here's your first chit. You'll want to hold on to that and get as many as you can during the conference." Joyce and I exchanged glances because we had no idea what she was talking about or even what a chit was. Of course, I decided I needed to have a little piece of laminated paper, too, so I said to my greeter, "Uh, I didn't get a chit." She smiled sweetly and said, "No, you didn't." I wanted to smack her, but I stayed true to my goal. "Say," I said just as sweetly, "what's all this about anyway?" She just grinned slyly and said, "Oh, don't ask any questions. You'll find out when we want you to know." And I definitely would have smacked her then if Joyce hadn't dragged me away.

As it turned out, the "chits" were little token awards the facilitators at the conference handed out at will to reward participants for arbitrary and capricious choices of the benefactors. One group leader passed out chits to everyone who arrived on time for a workshop. The next leader gave out chits to everyone who wore pink that day. Somehow, Joyce kept raking in the chits, and I got zip. Being the professional I am, by Day 2, I sat in the back of each training session alternately pouting and seething. At one point, I looked up and saw a bunch of teachers jumping up and down like they were on *Let's Make a Deal* trying to get the leader's attention so they could win a chit. I steamed as I thought, "This is the most demeaning, disrespectful thing these workshop facilitators are doing. They've got professional teachers begging for those stupid little chits like a bunch of trained seals. This is disgusting."

And then it hit me. How was this any different than what I was doing with my Super Citizen Awards at school? Wasn't I being just as manipulative and controlling? And I wondered if any of my students ever felt about me as I felt about those facilitators. That day started a revelation for me. In case you are wondering what the chits were about, on the last day of the conference we were asked to line up by the number of chits we had accumulated during the training. There were more than 100 of us. Joyce was somewhere near the front, so she got to go early to the prize table to choose her reward. She got a cassette player for her classroom. I was last in line because I had no chits. By the time I got to the table, the only thing left was pad and a pencil with the organization's logo on it. As I picked them up, I tossed my head into the air and announced, "At least I have my pride!" (Okay, maybe I didn't say it aloud, but in my head, I said it.)

My Reward Fiasco

One other incident cemented my shattered love affair with rewards. I was a guest speaker in a middle school doing a science discussion with about 50 students in their commons area. I was there to demonstrate exciting science phenomena, show and talk about my snake, and engage the kids in lively conversations about science topics. Because I wasn't there to evaluate or grade them, I had little trouble getting them to answer questions and speculate aloud about a range of subjects. They were totally engaged. And then I ruined it. One young man answered a question with such perceptive insight that my jaw almost hit the floor. I was so overwhelmed by the unexpected depth of his answer I unthinkingly reached in my pocket, pulled out a piece of bubblegum, threw it to him, and declared, "Wow, that answer is worth a prize!" That's all it took. It was my undoing. Kids who before were polite and respectful of one another started pushing and shoving trying to get my attention. They yelled out anything they could think of to try to win a piece of gum. They sulked when I didn't call on them, and they were less than courteous to me and to one another. And the worst thing was I had no way to undo it.

I managed to turn a wonderful time of exchanging ideas, enjoying natural phenomena, and informally interacting with kids into a circus of screaming preadolescents whose only focus was on winning a piece of bubblegum. Another lesson learned.

Varying Degrees of Rewards

I have made many mistakes as a parent and a teacher, but at least I am a reflective practitioner. I really try to grow by thinking deeply about which practices work and which ones don't. I also read and listen to what other people have to say.

After the science seminar calamity, I finally read Alfie Kohn's (1993) milestone book *Punished by Rewards* and was surprised by how much of what he has to say finally made sense to me. While I don't agree with everything Mr. Kohn advocates regarding rewards and kids, I find his arguments to be thought provoking, and I agree with him on more issues than not. As I continued my study of rewards, and I came across some very distinct differences among external rewards.

TYPES OF EXTERNAL REWARDS

- **Task-contingent rewards** are available to students for merely participating in an activity without regard to any standard of performance (e.g., Anyone who turns in a homework paper gets an A. Everybody on the team gets a trophy for something. The only measure of merit is how long workers have been employed.)
- **Performance-contingent rewards** are available only when the student achieves a certain standard (e.g., Anyone who has at least 93% correct responses on the homework paper gets a prize).
- **Success-contingent rewards** are given for good performance and might reflect either success or progress toward a goal (e.g., Anyone who has at least 93% correct responses on the homework paper or improves his last score by at least 10% receives a prize).

Task contingency is solely focused on compliance. "You do this, and I'll do that." No attention is paid to the quality of the job or the effort that went into the task. Unfortunately, our goal for their compliance is often grounded in a covert bargain that they will get what they want if we get what we want. External cunning or pressure can sometimes bring about compliance, but with acquiescence comes various negative consequences, including an urge to defy.

Most researchers agree that task-contingent rewards are at best futile and at worst counterproductive. There are varying opinions about the need for either performance-contingent rewards or success-contingent reward, but at least success-contingent rewards give everyone a reasonable chance.

Paul Chance, The Voice of Reason

Unlike Mr. Kohn, I was not convinced I had to get rid of all rewards. Sometimes, I feel I need something in my cache when I work with extremely disruptive kids who are out of control before I even start. I need some way of getting them to internalize a few restraints so they can at least hear what I have to say. I found an article by Paul Chance (1992) to be extremely helpful. Here is an adaptation of his suggested guidelines:

GUIDELINES FOR USING CLASSROOM REWARDS

- Use the weakest reward required to strengthen a behavior. (Don't give candy if a sticker will do. Don't give a sticker if praise will do.)
- When possible, avoid using rewards as incentives (task contingent).
- Reward at a high rate in the early stages of learning and reduce the frequency of rewards as students internalize behaviors that allow them to focus.
- Reward only the behavior you want repeated. (If you reward a long, verbose paper, expect to see lots more of them.)
- Remember that what is an effective reward for one student may not work well with another.

(Continued)

(Continued)

- Reward success, and set standards so that success is within *each* student's grasp.
- Bring attention to the rewards (both intrinsic and extrinsic) that are available for students from sources other than the teacher (other students, parents, or school personnel).
- Continually work toward a system that uses less-extrinsic rewards.

I like the idea of moving away from extrinsic rewards because there is extensive research pointing to their lack of effectiveness. In hundreds of studies, the conclusion is that rewards may temporarily (but not always) increase desired results, but long term, they have the opposite effect. Studies by Deci (1995); Ryan and Deci (2000a); Lepper, Greene, and Nibbet (1973); Ames (1990); and Rowe (1987) found that removing a reward extinguishes the behavior.

In other words, once a reward is given for a behavior, subsequent removal of that reward will cause the participant to lose interest or quit. Lepper, Greene, and Nibbet (1973) caused a dramatic loss of interest in drawing with markers by first rewarding young children for using them and then withdrawing the reward.

Pink (2009) reports that neuroscientists have found the use of contingent rewards can be as potentially addictive as alcohol and other drugs. In MRI scans, they have observed brain behavior when subjects are offered a chance to win money or other rewards. Pink cites a study by Knutson, Adams, Fong, and Hommer (2001) at Stanford University, which reports that during anticipation of rewards the brain chemical dopamine surges through a part of the brain called the nucleus accumbens. The feeling is delightful but soon dissipates demanding another dose. Pink concludes that

By offering a reward, a principal [someone in power] signals to the agent [the subordinate] that the task is undesirable. (If the task were desirable, the agent wouldn't need to prod.) . . . There's no going back. Pay your son to take out the trash—and you've pretty much guaranteed the kid will never do if again for free. What's more, once the money buzz tapers off, you'll likely have to increase the payment to continue the compliance. (p. 54)

Lepper, Greene, and Nisbett (1973), and later Deci (1995), write that careful consideration of the reward effects reported in 128 experiments clearly show that tangible rewards tend to have substantially negative effects on intrinsic motivation. The Jewish folktale about the old man and his handling of local ruffians (in this chapter's opening story) gives an illustration of the researchers' conclusions.

Rewards can limit the breadth of our thinking and can also reduce the depth of our thinking. Deci (1995) concludes that external rewards all too often get people focused only on outcomes, and that leads to shortcuts, which may be undesirable. He states that people offered rewards frequently take the shortest or quickest path to get them, often sacrificing deeper meaning. (See the question about schoolwide incentives in Chapter 10.)

In his book *Drive*, Pink (2009) concludes his views on rewards and punishments with his seven deadly flaws of carrots and sticks:

CARROTS AND STICKS: THE SEVEN DEADLY FLAWS

1. They can extinguish intrinsic motivation.
2. They can diminish performance.
3. They can crush creativity.
4. They can crowd out good behavior.
5. The can encourage cheating, shortcuts, and unethical behavior.
6. They can become addictive.
7. They can foster short-term thinking.

Source: Pink, 2009, p. 59.

Praise as a Reward

I have wrestled with Alfie Kohn's (1993) contention that most everything an adult does overtly to affirm a student has negative consequences. For instance, Kohn believes that every kind of positive reinforcer undermines the learner's intrinsic motivation. In his numerous works, Mr. Kohn expounds on his theory that any type of positive recognition should be viewed with skepticism. He warns that adults need to refrain from not only the use of stars, stickers, and other tangible compensations, but also from intangibles such as nods, smiles, pats, thumbs-up, and/or any type of reinforcement. Personally, I think that sometimes a pat on the back, a wink, or a nod does wonders to reassure a child who is struggling or who just needs to know someone is paying attention.

It is Kohn's (1993) belief that any form of demonstrative behavior that ties a learner to the approval of the adult is a form of coercive behaviorism that ultimately destroys the learner's self-efficacy. I wouldn't go that far, but I do agree that sometimes statements made to students in the guise of positive affirmations are actually just manipulative controls used to get the child to conform to the adult's desires.

Example

The teacher walks over to a child who is sitting quietly and says with a big smile, "I love the way you are behaving yourself. You have made me really happy with how good you are being today!" The teacher then pats the child on the back.

In this example, it is Kohn's conviction that the teacher has just communicated to the child that it is the child's job to please the teacher. The smile and the pat also reinforce the idea that when the child demonstrates the desired behavior, approval and acceptance will follow. Kohn (1993) contends that even if the smile and the pat are given without verbal summary, the child gets the idea that the point of behaving well is to please the teacher. He prefers the teacher ignores the child and lets the child experience the natural consequences of demonstrating appropriate behavior and not the reward of the teacher's positive attention. Kohn's belief is that by rewarding the positive behavior choices with words, a smile, and a pat, the teacher has taken the intrinsic reward of making the right choice away from the student and has made the student dependent on the teacher for extrinsic reward. I find it difficult not to affirm students openly, but Kohn's work has caused me to reconsider some of my word choices.

I started thinking how many "I statements" I used when praising students. "I like the way you answered that." "See this smile? Your positive attitude just put the happy back in my face." "Whenever I catch you being good, I'll give you a reward." Yep, it was all about me. Inadvertently, I was telling students it was their job to make me happy rather than focusing them on the important concepts of self-efficacy and autonomy.

I have tried very hard over the past few years to modify my comments and make them more student-centered (e.g., "You must feel really proud of the choice you made." "How does it feel to try so hard to accomplish something and then finally do it?" "Tell me why you chose that particular topic to write about.") Changing the way I praise has not been easy. I still slip with an occasional "I love it when you use your good manners" to my grandchildren, but I am very much aware of what I say to learners now and am more diligent about choosing my words.

Kohn (1993) believes we may be creating "praise junkies" out of our children. I've certainly done my part of that. My natural enthusiasm makes many of my remarks seem extremely amplified and way too effusive. It's hard to maintain that over-the-top pep all the time, and researchers say it would be far better to make neither derisive nor effusive comments. Simple feedback and getting the child to answer questions about her work is much preferred. Kohn (2001) offers the following alternatives to the ubiquitous "Good Job!" parents and teachers say almost automatically these days.

ALTERNATIVE TO SAYING "GOOD JOB!"

1. **Say nothing.** Sometimes praise calls attention to something that does not need it. Overzealous praise may give the child the idea that you think the positive behavior is a fluke.

2. **Say what you saw.** A simple evaluation-free acknowledgment lets the child know you noticed. "You went the extra mile in helping your friend." "You did it!" Or describe what you see. "Wow, you've got this room looking like a professional housekeeper was here."

3. **Talk less, ask more.** Better than describing is asking questions about the work. "So what made you decide to clean your room like this?" "How did you select such an interesting topic to write about?"

Source: Adapted from Kohn, 2001.

No More Stars, Stickers, or Trophies? Really?

Kohn (1993) cites study after study on intrinsic motivation to make his points. However, others who have analyzed the same studies come up with somewhat different conclusions. In 2001, Marzano, Pickering, and Pollack, well-known educational researchers, examined numerous investigations and arrived at this determination, "Rewards—particularly praise—when given for accomplishing specific performance goals, can be a powerful motivator for students" (p. 58). Their reasoning is when teachers and parents focus on progress toward success (i.e., for accomplishing specific performance goals) and use recognition rather than rewards, the results can lead to positive motivation for the child:

> Reinforcing effort can help teach students one of the most valuable lessons they can learn—the harder you try, the more successful you are. In addition, providing recognition for attainment of specific goals not only enhances achievement, but it stimulates motivation. (p. 59)

I'm glad to know that because personally I like stars, stickers, and trophies when they are use appropriately and prudently.

Motivating Kids to Do Unexciting Tasks

Other researchers agree that appropriate use of rewards is not always debilitating and can sometimes yield some very positive outcomes in other ways. Pink (2009) concludes that "For routine tasks, which aren't very interesting and don't demand much creative thinking, rewards can provide a small booster shot without harmful side effects" (p. 62).

The logic behind that statement is that you cannot undermine someone's intrinsic motivation if the job requires little or no intrinsic motivation in the first place. Pink (2009) justifies using task contingent rewards in such a circumstance. He offers these tips to make the job more palatable:

HOW TO ENCOURAGE LEARNERS WHEN THE TASK AT HAND IS BORING OR ROUTINE

1. Offer a rational explanation of why the task is necessary (e.g., *"Diagramming sentences may seem pointless to you right now, but I promise you, it will*

(Continued)

(Continued)

eventually strengthen your writing skills. Let me give you an example." "Doing these sprints will build your stamina so that you will be a stronger player in the long run." "Once you commit your multiplication tables to memory, you won't have to waste time calculating them in your head, and you'll find that math is a whole lot easier for you.").

2. Acknowledge that the task is boring (e.g., *"Yeah, I don't like this part either. It seems so dull and repetitive. However, everyone who has ever succeeded in this had to do the same thing we're doing." "Okay, let's get this part over with so we can get on to the fun stuff." "I play little games with myself to make this part less boring. Let me show you one you might like to try.").*

3. Allow learners to complete the task in their own way (e.g., *"Maybe you would like to do this to music or perhaps do a little rap as you work." "You can do this in the morning or in the evening—whatever works best for you." "Sure, you can do the practice steps backward. That should be interesting.").*

Source: Adapted from Pink, 2009.

I'm quite sure Alfie Kohn would ask, "Why are we asking kids to do trivial, mundane tasks in the first place? Shouldn't we put our efforts into making every task more interesting and engaging?" Like most parents and teachers, I do my very best to ensure that tasks and lessons are as engaging as humanly possible, but I think sometimes we just have to admit that some perfunctory requirements and rudimentary tasks are just boring, and it's better to figure out the most engaging way to deal with those.

Rewards as Affirmations

Teresa Amabile (1996), professor at the Harvard Business School, has done considerable research on rewards and their effect on creativity. She and her colleagues have determined that an extrinsic reward can have positive impact if it is unexpected and offered only after the task is complete (e.g., giving someone a certificate of appreciation after they have designed the school's logo as a congratulatory symbol of achievement rather than offering the task-contingent proviso "If you design an incredible logo, then you get a prize."). Amabile also advises adults to consider keeping the rewards nontangible. She and Deci (1995) concur that positive feedback, used appropriately, can improve intrinsic motivation. They believe that recognition that confirms competence can be extremely effective. I am glad about that. I love praise when it is earned—both receiving it and giving it. Nonetheless, Alfie Kohn, Carol Dweck, and others have taught me to use my praise more judiciously.

Conclusion

I think the use of rewards is a complicated issue that must be seriously considered and reconsidered by parents and teachers alike. I don't believe there is any single right answer to how much, how often, or what kinds of rewards are appropriate for all children at all times. I still struggle with this issue. Nevertheless, my research and my experiences have led me to believe that usually less is more. Sometimes the simple act of giving children our full attention is the most effective way to support them. Helping them learn to attribute success to their effort is a compelling life lesson. And reminding children they have choices strengthens their sense of autonomy. Chapter 7 deals with the theory of autonomy along with other tools that help students thrive.

Autonomy, Time, and Flow

. . . .

Listen to the desires of your children. Encourage them and then give them the autonomy to make their own decisions.

—Denis Waitley

. . . .

Chapter 6 outlines several drawbacks to the inappropriate use of extrinsic rewards as motivators. An additional consequence of extrinsic rewards is that they often rob students of their *autonomy,* or the right (or power) to govern themselves. This chapter considers the elements of autonomy and their impact on successful living. How much choice we have in how we spend our time is a significant factor in the amount of autonomy we feel. Careful attention to time allocation is also a strategy for helping learners wrestle with difficult concepts and tasks. And as it turns out, time has a tremendous influence on the ultimate state of intrinsic motivation, *flow.*

Autonomy

Autonomy is an essential component of self-motivation because it is a vital part of what empowers learners to act. The belief that one's choices and efforts make a difference is grounded in the assumption that one has at least partial authority over his environment. Edward Deci (1995) says autonomy is an important part of *self-determination*. He believes children perceive their circumstances as either as autonomous or as *controlled*. With a perception of autonomy, individuals are willing to do what they are doing and embrace the activity with a sense of interest and commitment. If the situation is perceived as controlling, people act without a sense of personal endorsement; they feel manipulated.

More From The Tiger Mom

Amy Chua (2011), self-described "Tiger Mom," writes in her article for *The Wall Street Journal* that neither of her two daughters were ever allowed to

- attend a sleepover,
- have a play date,
- be in a school play,
- complain about not being in a school play,
- watch TV or play computer games,
- choose their own extracurricular activities,
- get any grades less than an A, and
- *not* be the best student in every subject except gym or drama.

She goes on to discuss how for the most part Eastern parents care nothing about making learning fun and believe it is the child's job to make her parents proud through demonstrated achievement.

Ms. Chua (2011) states that Eastern children are required to master either violin or piano. No other instrument is acceptable. She says that being in a school play is a waste of a child's time. She asks why a child should be content to be a "Villager Number Six" and expect the parent to provide transportation to and from afterschool practice for that. Her inference is the child could be at home doing long hours of practice toward something more achievement oriented.

Ms. Chua (2011) purports it is the Eastern parent's duty to bully, coerce, and insult their children to make sure they eventually succeed. She believes that parents should sacrifice their lives to engineer their offspring's success, and children owe their parents everything in return.

I know and have taught many Eastern children who have been highly successful in school. For years, I have counseled both Eastern and Western parents that while it is reasonable and desirable to ask that a child *do* her best, it is not reasonable, nor desirable, to ask a child to *be* the best. My first thought about Ms. Chua's article is that in a classroom full of Eastern children, how can every student be the best? In my view, berating a child for being second or third or fourth seems over the top. To me, the notion that only the parent selects the child's extracurricular activities devalues the whole idea of play and childhood. It certainly undermines autonomy.

I am troubled by Ms. Chua's idea that a parent of a child who is gaining too much weight should say, "You are a disgrace because you are fat; you are an embarrassment to this family. From now on, I will decide what you can and cannot eat." I have to admit, though, Western parents are sometimes too ambivalent with our children: "Honey, I really think you would be healthier and happier if you ate less ice cream, but it's up to you to make that decision for yourself. I know you really want ice cream right now, so maybe just this once. Do you want chocolate syrup on top?" Perhaps, there is some middle ground in there somewhere.

I think parents must set limits when it comes to issues that deal with health and safety. But, unlike Ms. Chua, I think, more times than not, it benefits children to make them partners in decision making. I believe our goal should be to rear children who realize they have competence and should have a voice in what affects them.

Promoting Autonomy in Learners

Students who feel empowered by a sense of autonomy are far more likely to stay with an activity or a task and gain more from it long term (Ryan & Deci, 2000b). The standard reactions to excessive control are both undesirable—unthinking compliance and/or defiance. Effective educators concerned with student engagement are always quick to point out that students need ownership in what they are learning. Learners are more likely to be self-motivated and have greater task satisfaction if they feel they have at least some degree of control.

Autonomy does not necessarily mean that one has to strictly "go it alone." But rather, it means that one is acting with a sense of choice and volition. This can happen simultaneously while one is enjoying interdependence with others.

Since autonomous behavior is associated with richer experience, better conceptual understanding, greater creativity, and improved problem solving (Ryan & Deci, 2000b), it is important that parents and teachers ensure certain conditions are met to provide students with a sense of personal freedom. You will note that most of these conditions are also necessary to promote concepts previously mentioned in this book: growth mindset, self-efficacy, and lifelong learning.

PROMOTING AUTONOMY IN LEARNERS

1. Provide the learner with choice.

"You can choose how you would like to demonstrate what you learned from the book you read. Feel free to select a written report, a PowerPoint demonstration, a monologue performance, a background musical score you create for the different chapters, or something else you would like to use. Here's the rubric I'll be using to assess your understanding. Just let me know which method you plan to use."

"Each family member is responsible for contributing to the overall quality of life in this house. Your father and I have certain things we do, and we expect you children to

do the same. Write five things you are willing to do each week that will benefit the other family members."

"Committing your multiplication tables to memory will be highly beneficial to you not only now but for the rest of your life. Do you want to practice them with flash cards, work on a game at the computer, write them several times each, use these art supplies to illustrate them, or have me call them out to you? You can pick a different method tomorrow, but for now which way do you want to practice?"

2. Encourage students to experiment, do creative thinking, and challenge themselves.

"That's an interesting question you asked about the science experiment we just did. How would you go about finding out the answer? If I help you round up the materials you need, do you want to test your hypothesis?"

"Wow! That was some exceptional dribbling I saw you do. Can you do the same thing with your other hand?"

"You're right about the math discovery you made. However, it isn't really a coincidence. Everything in math has a reason behind it. Can you come up with a math theory that explains why it always turns out that way?"

"That was a concise summary of The Hunger Games. *Suzanne Collins has said that the premise for the book came to her one evening when she was channel surfing and flipped from a reality-television competition to footage from the war in Iraq. Can you explain how that combination may have influenced her novel?"*

3. Focus the student in the student's zone of proximal development.

"Oh wow! You finished already? Let me see that. It looks as though I just wasted your time by giving you something you already knew how to do. I apologize. Why don't you try this next activity and see if it challenges you."

(Continued)

(Continued)

"You know what? I think you're getting confused by trying to do too many steps at once. Let's return to the one-step solutions and let you get confident with that before we move to multiple steps. See how you do with these one-step problems."

"Yes, I can see you're really putting a lot of effort into these problems, and look at you getting them right! Don't worry about how long it's taking. We can adjust for that. Just keep doing what you're doing. Remember, you did it once, and you can do it again."

4. Provide feedback that is nonjudgmental and gives specific information about how to improve.

"You will probably find it easier to keep up with your decimal places if you concentrate on keeping your numbers in straight vertical lines. Let me give you a piece of graph paper to help you line up your numbers in a symmetrical way. See if that doesn't make it a little easier to keep up with where the decimals go."

"When you're playing outfield you need to keep your body ready to move as soon as the ball is hit. Try it again, but this time loosen up your body and be ready to run the second the batter contacts the ball. Let me show you what I mean. Now, you do it."

"On this test question you got the right answer, but you did not give any supporting details. Part of what I am trying to assess is how much you understand about what was happening at this time in history. Take your paper back and write down at least three reasons the soldiers made the decision they did. If you don't know, you may need to reread the account in your text or see what you can find out on the Internet."

5. Give meaningful reasons for the task.

"The reason we are practicing using a Thesaurus is because it is a helpful resource to improve your writing.

> *Learning to use the exact word you need adds tremendous impact to your ability to tell a story. Let me read you two paragraphs—one, a student wrote before using a Thesaurus and the second one after she used one. You tell me about any differences you notice."*
>
> *"Multiplying fractions may not seem useful to you now, but let me show you a slide presentation of just a few instances most people need that knowledge. Watch for what kinds of jobs use that skill on a daily basis."*
>
> *"The reason you need to feed the dog close to the same time every day is that he's depending on you for his nourishment. His biological clock alerts him when it's time to eat, and he's helpless to do anything about it. I know you enjoy the special relationship you have with your dog, and I know you want to be the one who sees that he gets what he needs when he needs it."*

Promoting autonomy in learners gives them a sense of control over their world, and we've already examined how important it is for them to feel they have power over their lives. It is crucial to note that autonomy does not mean permissiveness. Rather, it is more of a negotiation between the adult and the learner that is flexible and proactive. The adult, of course, must set limits, but that can be done effectively by keeping limits as wide as possible, explaining the reasons for the limits, and avoiding controlling language. Deci (1995) explains the difference in autonomy-supportive and conventional-controlling language in the following scenario. He is describing an experiment carried out by two of his associates:

He [Richard Ryan] worked with Richard Koestner and identified a classic situation requiring both limits and creative autonomy: children's art. The idea was to engage kids (five- and six-year-olds) in a creative but potentially messy task of painting a picture. Limits concerning neatness were set up in two different ways—the conventional controlling way, and a non-controlling, autonomy-supportive way. The controlling way was simple: use pressuring language ("Be a good boy/girl and keep the materials neat," or "Do as you should, and don't mix up the colors.") . . .

In the autonomy-supportive limits group the researcher said, "I know that sometimes it's really fun to just slop the paint around, but here the materials and room need to be kept nice for the other children who will use them. (1995, pp. 42–43)

Deci (1995) reports the difference between the two groups was dramatic. The autonomy-supportive statement seemed to have an energizing effect on the children while the controlling statement had the opposite effect. The children who felt the adults understood them were far more intrinsically motivated and enthusiastic than were the children in the other group. It is important to note that the researchers found a way to encourage responsibility without undermining motivation. According to Deci,

Limit setting is extremely important for promoting responsibility, and the findings of this study are critical for how to do it. By setting limits in an autonomy-supportive way—in other words, by aligning yourself with the person being limited, recognizing that he or she is a proactive subject, rather than an object to be manipulated or controlled—it is possible to encourage responsibility without undermining authenticity. (p. 43)

The following are some examples of how these different languages might sound in a classroom:

IT'S ALL IN THE WAY YOU SAY IT: SUPPORTING AUTONOMY WITHOUT DEMOTIVATING

Controlling–C
Autonomy Supportive–AS

C: *"You can work in groups as long as you stay on task and don't get too loud."*

AS: *"It's fun to laugh and talk with friends, but make sure your volume doesn't bother other groups. You can have a good time and still get the job done."*

C: *"You can use the Internet, but be sure you only go to sites that are school approved and are directly related to your topic."*

AS: *"You're a responsible person, so I'm sure you'll use the Internet wisely. Isn't it great to be able to search for information about your topic that's not just available in the textbook? Let me know if you find something unique."*

C: *"You can clean out the hamster cage as long as you follow the guidelines you see posted there. Make sure you don't let the hamster loose, and clean up your mess when you are done."*

AS: *"I really appreciate your volunteering to help take care of our hamster. That was always a fun thing for me to do when I was a student. Where are you planning on putting Scruffy while you clean the cage? If you need some tips for cleaning, just take a peek at that list on the wall. It's there for backup if you need it."*

In my experience, the heart of building autonomy lies in giving students meaningful choices and being responsive to them as learners. Nel Noddings (1992) writes, "We cannot enter into dialogue with children when we know that our decision is already made" (p. 23). That does not mean that teachers and parents have to give choices on every issue. We just have to make sure that when the opportunity presents itself we include the student in the decision making. Everyone likes to have a voice; giving children a genuine opportunity to be heard is critical to helping them build their self-efficacy. Parents of younger children sometimes need to limit choices, such as the following:

- *"It's a little cold outside this morning, so do you want to wear your brown sweater or your red coat?"*
- *"For dinner, you can have macaroni and cheese with a salad or with mixed vegetables. You'll want to fill up because the next available food is tomorrow at breakfast."*
- *"Do you want to write your thank-you note to Grandma tonight or tomorrow morning before you go out to play?"*
- *"It's time for homework. Do you want to start with math or social studies?"*

In this way, the adults can set up certain parameters, but the child still gets to have a say. Some of you are probably wondering, "What do I do if the child says she doesn't want to do either of the choices?" An appropriate response to prevent delaying tactics would be, "Okay, you seem to be having trouble making up your mind. In 15 seconds, you choose or I choose for you."

Stepping In Too Quickly

Supporting autonomy includes using strategies such as encouraging students to solve their problems. Negotiating with children takes a lot of time and patience, and sometimes adults want to shortcut the process by simply taking over the task. For some adults, it's about impatience, but for others, such as Amy Chua, it's about control. Occasionally, parents and teachers are driven by forces other than what is in the best interest of the child (e.g., "I just want to get this over with." "She's going to embarrass me in front of everyone." "If I make him do this, he's going to pout all night." "I'm too tired to deal with this.")

Other times, it's just a matter of not thinking cogently about our long-term goals for the learner. When teachers immediately jump in to assist the student, they rob her of the opportunity to wrestle with an intellectual ambiguity that may eventually strengthen her reasoning. We are not allowing her to become an independent thinker, and therefore, we inhibit her potential. We should not be doing things for students they can do for themselves. If they cannot do it, we need to teach them the tools they need so they can.

As a teacher, I know that I stepped in too quickly for some students after asking them a question in class. The student would look at me with that deer-in-the-headlights look, and I would worry that I was going to somehow traumatize him if I didn't quickly ask another student to help. What I came to realize is when I did that I was virtually telling every person in the classroom, including the recipient of my question, that I didn't think he could do it. I also was giving him a terrific lesson in learned helplessness (i.e., *If I just look wide-eyed and keep quiet, she'll move on, and I won't have to think*). Only after studying the research on *wait time* did I begin to understand that I needed to wait at least three to seven seconds for a response. At that point, rather than moving away from the student, I needed to provide cues, prompts, and further questions to help clarify the answer. Like most teachers, I made my decisions based on the best intentions. I didn't want the student to be embarrassed. I thought I was rescuing him. But now, *I'm* embarrassed by all those missed opportunities to help my reluctant participants gain a little autonomy.

When adults rush in to repair the collapsed craft-stick bridge, to take charge of the science fair project, to do the math problems, to rewrite part of the essay, or in any other way intervene in students' work, we send a clear message to them that we do not see them as competent. We do not trust them to clean up their messes, and we do not want to give up control. It is important to give feedback, to create a positive environment for children to do their assignments, and to listen to them work through their dilemmas. Helping them explore choices and possible outcomes is an effective way to teach them self-efficacy and autonomy. It does not, however, teach students to have self-efficacy, autonomy, or a growth mindset if we fail to turn over appropriate power to them and give them a chance to test their wings. That's how this Western mom sees it anyway.

WAIT TIME

Studies beginning in the early 1970s and continuing through the 1980s show that if teachers pause between three and seven seconds after asking higher-level questions, students respond with more thoughtful answers. This finding is consistent at the elementary, middle school, and high school levels.

Increasing the wait time from three to seven seconds results in an increase in (1) the length of student responses, (2) the number of unsolicited responses, (3) the frequency of student questions, (4) the number of responses from less-capable children, (5) student-to-student interactions, and (6) the incidence of speculative responses. In addition to pausing after asking questions, research shows that many of these same benefits result when teachers pause after the student's response to a question and when teachers do not affirm answers immediately (Rowe, 1987).

Time Allocation

As adults, we sometimes underestimate the power of time. Giving children a certain amount of choice about how they spend their time is critical to helping them establish their autonomy. However, time allocation is a frequently overlooked strategy for helping learners become successful. One of the single most demotivating conditions for learners is when they feel they don't have enough time to do what is asked of them. I have seen many a student crumple an assignment or snap a pencil in frustration when they realize they are not able to do what is asked of them in the time given. Thoughtful, purposeful allocation of time is a tool that requires no additional training or materials, and yet few adults take advantage of this important tactic.

In a recent presentation, I made the statement that timing nonmastery learners was a kind of professional malfeasance. The audience gasped when I said it. I know what they were thinking, "But what about those timed tests the state makes us give all learners? We are required to give them. We have to time learners to get ready for them." Do we?

In an age where advanced brain research has vividly depicted that undue anxiety limits cognitive transfer, how can we justify adding more stress to learners by timing them and then reporting their intellectual achievement levels by how many correct answers they managed to retrieve from their stored knowledge base under duress? Think about it. Have you ever had something slip just beyond your conscious recall when you were struggling to remember it? Did stress help you access that particular piece of information, or did it just cause it to slip even further from retrieval? And what happened the minute the opportunity passed or the stress was otherwise removed? You remembered it, didn't you? You knew it all along, but you just couldn't gain access to it at that particular moment because of the barrier of angst.

Some would argue that part of mastery is being able to recall or perform under duress. I agree. When students have mastered a concept or a skill, we need to challenge them in all sorts of ways. In fact, doing timed tests is one way to move a student from mastery into *automaticity*, the ability to perform certain functions without conscious effort. It allows students to move on to higher-order functions without having to stop and think about every sequence in rudimentary steps. But a nonmastery learner is not yet to that point, and adding the burden of performing under the stress of being timed seems incongruent with the goal of giving every learner a reasonable chance at success.

Carol Ann Tomlinson (Sousa & Tomlinson, 2011) recommends differentiating instruction through content, process, product, and affect/environment. Part of her design for differentiating process is for teachers to vary the time they allow individual students to work on their assignments. Struggling learners are granted more time to practice and work through the basics. Mastery learners are granted more time to pursue their interests or to extend their learning. Teachers are encouraged to use time both as an instructional and a management tool.

Parents and teachers can effectively use time limits to minimize delaying tactics from reluctant children. They can help students make responsible choices by creating timelines for long-term assignments and goals. And most important, they can discuss the time constraints with learners to ensure that they are equitable and are fully understood. The optimal learning environment has a great deal to do with time.

Optimal Learning Environment and Flow

Beginning in the 1970s, University of Chicago psychologist Mihalyi Csikszentmihalyi (1997) began to examine the optimal learning environment. His studies led him to believe it is one in which "a person's skills are fully involved in overcoming a challenge that is just about manageable" (p. 30). Are you beginning to sense a theme here—Vygotsky, Deci, Ericsson, Dweck, and now Csikszentmihalyi?

Csikszentmihalyi (1997) was curious about the state of mind that occurs when a high-level achiever is engaged in a high-functioning task. He coined the term "flow" to refer to a state of highly concentrated action and awareness. In sports terms, it's what an athlete would call "being in the zone." It is the epitome of intrinsic motivation because the total reward is performing the act itself. Self-consciousness fades away, and a solidarity of focus ensues. Research participants describe flow as a state of being so engaged in an activity (e.g., running, writing, exploring, painting, dancing, performing, reading) that the senses of time, space, and outside stimuli are temporarily suspended. Study subjects report that when they are in this depth of concentration they feel energized and euphoric. They compare the feeling to being carried by a current, everything moving smoothly without effort (Silver, 2005, p. 122).

Being in a Flow State

Think about instances in your life where you were so engaged, so caught up with what you were doing that you lost track of time, you forgot to eat, you were oblivious to the world around you, and you were having the time of your life. You were in what Csikszentmihalyi (1997) describes as a flow state. Consider athletes who are so focused on doing what they do best that they don't even realize they have been injured in the process. In the state of flow, people often feel euphoric, energized, and totally aligned with the task.

In his book *The Pistol: The Life of Pete Maravich*, biographer Mark Kriegel (2007) details how the iconic player reached epic proportions in his ability to handle a basketball and do things on court that had never been done before. Throughout his life, even as a very young boy, Pete was able to reach such a state of focus and concentration that he figuratively "entered his own world" when he handled a basketball. People had to remind him to eat, drink, and sleep because his single-minded dedication to the game of basketball often consumed his conscious thought.

My stepson Andy is like that when he plays his drums. He can practice for hours on end with such determined attention that he doesn't hear the phone ring, feel the need for food, or mind the time he spends sitting in his music room while his friends are at the lake or attending a ball game. It looks like hard work to me, but he calls it bliss.

Adults can help students become aware of flow state by pointing out instances they recognize it in students or see it evidenced by a third party, say in a movie or when observing an expert doing what she does best. We can plan for prolonged periods in which students are free to engage fully with their respective areas of interest. Having extended time to fully interact with, explore, and practice their interests helps promote the flow state.

Glenn Derry and *Avatar*

When I was a classroom teacher, I had never heard of "flow state" or Csizkszentmihalyi. I realized that some of my students got so involved in their science explorations that they were disappointed when the bell rang to change classes. One child in particular comes to mind, Glenn Derry. Glenn often complained that the cooperative group I put him in disrupted his thinking. He demanded that I let him work by himself so that he could concentrate on what he was doing and finish his project. I told him that part of my goal for him was to teach him to collaborate with others and to learn to build consensus, both skills he would need for a successful future. He totally disagreed, but I knew I was doing what was best for him. Or at least, I thought I did.

At the end of the school year, Glenn's family moved back to their home state of California. I didn't hear from him for years. One day my son, Maverick, sent me a YouTube video he wanted me to see. It was an interview with James Cameron, director of *Avatar*, talking about his video engineer, Glenn Derry. In the interview, he explains that Glenn is the one who invented the camera that allowed *Avatar* to be made the way it was. In the interview, he states that to solve the problem, Glenn had to go away by himself, first for an hour and later for an entire year. When he (Glenn) came back, he had invented the camera Cameron needed. The way he solved the problem was to go to an isolated setting to totally focus on the problem and to have the freedom to work unimpeded. I cringed inwardly as remembered my words to my student in the sixth grade, "Glenn, you are never going to be successful unless you learn to work in a group." Oh my.

In all fairness to myself, I think that Glenn did need to learn to work with groups, at least, part of the time. However, if I had it to do over again, I would have said, "Glenn, you need to work in a group *for now*. For later, you will have the choice to work and think by yourself." In a conversation with my son, Glenn said that to solve the engineering problems he has confronted in the movies (e.g., *A.I., Jurassic Park III, Small Soldiers,* and *Avatar*—just to name a few), he has to get by himself where he can totally focus on the solution. I can just picture

Glenn in his workroom surrounded by gadgets and gizmos and in a total flow state, as he single-mindedly attends to the problem. It is comforting to know that some of my students succeeded in spite of my less-than-stellar insights. Thank goodness Glenn had enough autonomy to figure out what worked best for him.

> You can hear James Cameron's interview about Glenn Derry at http://www.youtube.com/watch?v=Aao0YSITuxc

Creating Flow in the Classroom

The state of "flow" does not occur naturally in a classroom. Bells, schedules, and other external forces work to disrupt attentive concentration. However, adults can help structure more opportunities for flow experiences. Csikszentmihalyi (1991) suggests these basic guidelines for those who wish to promote flow in the classroom:

TO HELP CREATE A SENSE OF FLOW

- Be sensitive to student's goals and desires; use this knowledge to choose and frame activities that provide meaningful challenges.
- Empower students to take control of their own learning by giving them freedom within the context of clearly articulated goals.
- Provide clear and immediate feedback to students about how they are doing without making them feel inadequate or self-conscious.
- Arrange for students to have appropriate time to focus, and help limit distractions.

The potential of reaching a flow state is often the validation needed to justify the repetitive tedium of learning and practicing basic skills we require of students. We can remind them that only when their fundamentals become automatic are they able to move into higher levels of performance and the extremely engaging flow states. And those are powerfully fun!

Helping Students Stay Motivated as They Get Older

. . . .
Our lives are shaped by those who love us, [and] those who refuse to love us.
—John Powell, professor of theology
. . . .

Chapter 8 is dedicated to helping children stay motivated and on track for a successful life as they get older. When we talk about older children, we are dealing with a vast range of ages, from preadolescence to preadult. I have taught every one of these age groups, and I am sometimes struck by their similarities as well as their dissimilarities. Inside even the most recalcitrant teenager, I often catch a glimpse of the little kid yelling, "Hey, did you see that? I *did* it!" Behind the blustery posturing of an eighth-grade "mean girl," I sometimes see the little girl inside asking, "Am I okay? Am I worthy? Will they figure out who I really am and hate me for it?" And even at the university level, I had a student who said, "Thanks for taking the time to write a personal note in my journal. It's nice to know that someone believes in me."

Most of what I've written about in this book is appropriate for any age level if attention is paid to their appropriate developmental stages. Many teachers and parents complain that it gets harder to keep kids motivated as they grow older. Research tells us that student motivation starts to wane in middle school and sometimes reaches a critical low in high school.

Part of this motivational dip may be explained by what happens to learners who have a fixed mindset and are experiencing setbacks for the first time in their lives, as the academic work gets progressively harder. Hormonal fluxes and social networking can also enter self-motivation lows during this period.

As habits become fixed, they become harder and harder to change. One thing to keep in mind is that changing a behavior usually takes about one month for every year since birth. For teachers who deal with kids older than nine, that can sound a little dismal since we only have an average of nine months total to influence a child. That is one of the reasons I'm such an advocate for a strong bond between schools and parents. Teachers can have a monumental sway with students, but we cannot do it alone. Likewise, parents can benefit from sharing advocacy for their children with the educators who are with their offspring most of their waking hours. I've always believed that if we adults could stick together—kids would win!

Procrastination

> *Putting off an easy thing makes it hard. Putting off a hard thing makes it impossible.*
>
> —George Claude Lorimer

One of the common problems occurring with older children is their tendency to procrastinate when they don't want to do something. Part of their delaying may stem from a need to tell the adults in their lives "You're not in charge of me. I may not be able to win an argument with you about this, but I can sure find a way to drag it out." The point is that true procrastination is needless and counterproductive. Often the student is actually worse off because of the deferral, and there's much time and energy wasted by both the adults and the children.

In his book *Do it Now: Break the Procrastination Habit*, William Knaus (1997) discusses methods for helping the procrastinator. Here are some ideas teachers and parents may find helpful in dealing with older students.

HELPING THE STUDENT WHO PROCRASTINATES

1. Ask the student to make a list of at least six things currently being put off: a book report, a science project, cleaning the garage, or whatever. (Having the reality of a definite list helps prevents the student from "just forgetting" about the various goals he has.)

2. Establish an objective, limited as it might be at first, for each of the delayed goals: write the first paragraph of the book report, make a materials list for the science project, clean one shelf in the garage. (Often, people just need an *action step* to get them started. Occasionally, *project inertia* will take care of the rest; sometimes it's just a matter of actively doing anything that triggers enough momentum to carry the learner forward.)

3. Ask the student to verbalize several affirming phrases: "It's just as hard to start tomorrow as it is today." "If I can take the first step, I can take the second." "Even if I don't yet have the ability to complete the task, I will develop my skills as I go along."

4. Let the student know that using cop-out statements such as "I guess I'm just lazy," or "I just

(Continued)

(Continued)

can't seem to make myself do it," are diversionary tactics and are unacceptable.

5. Convince the student that all the effort put into divertive tactics are signs of creativity and skill that could be put to better use toward solid academic gains. (I used to laugh at some of the extraordinary means my sons would use to get out of tasks and say, "Wow, if we could only channel those powers for good instead of evil!")

6. Pay attention to the completed goals, but don't overpraise or make too big a deal about it. (Get the student to focus on how he completed the action and what it felt like to finish it.)

Procrastination and the Zone of Proximal Development

Sometimes, procrastination builds to a critical mass, and the child cannot see how to solve the problem. Perhaps it's a matter of keeping her bedroom clean. The parent puts up with it until she just can't anymore. She loses it. She wants instant results and immediate conformity. But what will the child learn from that? She will probably just figure out that she can manage her life around mom's mood swings. Her life will be unbothered until Mom "throws one of her fits," and then she can manage by crisis. I think an assertive parent using the zone of proximal development (ZPD) can handle this problem in a reasonable way.

Scenario

Mom walks in to her teenage daughter's room and is furious to see that it is in shambles. Her daughter has been promising for weeks to get it cleaned up. The floor is strewn with clothes, food, makeup, CDs, and assorted trash. The closet looks like it just exploded, and bookshelf appears to have become a depository for every piece of "junk du jour" her daughter has ever collected. Her child is on the phone rolling her eyes at her mother's disconcerted look. Mom is fed up and decides that it is time for action.

Beyond ZPD

Mom: "Marley, get off that phone now. This room looks like a bomb went off in here. I swear the City Sanitation Department would condemn this place if they saw it. We could get this room on *Hoarders* if we called A&E. You've been promising to take care of this for weeks! Oh my goodness, I can't stand this! You have to clean it up from top to bottom right now! You are not going to leave this room until it is in perfect order. I want clothes picked up, folded, and hung up. I want all of the trash downstairs in the receptacle. Dirty dishes go to the kitchen. You need to clean out these drawers and get rid of the clothes you no longer wear. I want that bookshelf cleaned off and organized with books only! You need to vacuum this rug, change your linens, make your bed, clean your mirror, dust the furniture, and straighten up your desk. Now!"

Marley: "Mom, it's fine. All my friends keep their rooms the same way. I can find stuff when I really need it. I promise, I'll do it later. Besides, I wouldn't even know where to start."

Mom: "Well, you had better figure out where to start because you are not coming out of this room until I say it passes inspection, young lady!" As she exits the room she says, "Now get started and don't stop until I tell you to."

Marley: Gets up and slams the door. "Fine!"

Mom: Reopens door and slams it harder. "Fine!"

Later, Mom returns and sees virtually no progress. Marley is on the floor looking at a scrapbook she has uncovered. Mom informs her that she is grounded for life and storms out. Marley sits in the floor totally overwhelmed; she has no clue where to start and is having her own personal pity party over the injustice of it all. Mom sits in the kitchen seething over Marley's obstinate behavior. She cannot understand where she went wrong. The room remains a mess.

Not far enough for ZPD

Mom: "Oh, honey, look at this mess! How can you stand to live like this? I swear I don't know how you find anything! You really need to start being a little neater. I want you to clean up this entire room before you go to bed tonight. This time I mean it."

Marley: "Are you kidding me? That will take all night. I haven't even looked at my homework yet. And I'm hungry. I need something to eat. Mom, why are you being so mean? It's my room! I can't do all that stuff. It's too hard. Come on, Mom, I'm sorry. I'll start doing better. There's just no time to do all that now. I can't. I'm tired." Sniff, sniff. "Mom, I'm exhausted. I can't." Sob. "Way too much to ask!" Sob. "I'm can't do it by myself." Sniff. Sob.

Mom: Picking up clothes and starting to fold them. "Now, Marley, don't get upset. I know you are tired, and this probably is too big a job for you to do all by yourself. Do you think you could just gather all the dirty dishes and take them to the kitchen?"

Marley: "No, I can't carry all that stuff. I'll drop something. Could you do it for me? Please?"

Mom: "Well, okay, but why don't you just gather your dirty clothes and put them in the laundry basket?"

Marley: "I don't know what's clean and what's dirty. I guess I'll just put everything in the laundry."

Mom: "Oh no, honey, I don't want to wash clothes that are already clean. I tell you what; I'll hold up each piece and you can tell me if it is dirty or not. Would that work?"

Marley: "I guess, but Hilary is going to call me in a minute to talk about homework, so what do I do about that?"

Mom: "Well, you talk to Hilary, and I'll hold up each item of clothing. You can point to the laundry basket if it's dirty or shake your head if it's not. I can fold the clothes that are clean and put them where they belong, but this is the last time I am doing this, do you hear me?"

Marley: "Thanks, Mom. I could not clean my room without you."

Then Mom proceeds to clean the entire room for Marley. And she will continue to do so as long as she allows her young Blanche DuBois to shirk her responsibilities and play the "I'm so helpless" card.

Appropriate ZPD:

Mom: "Marley, I need you to wrap up that phone call so we can have a talk about something important."

Marley: Hanging up the phone. "Okay, what is it?"

Mom: "I want you to look around this room and tell me how it stacks up with our family guidelines for room responsibility."

Marley: "I know. I've let it go too long, and it's pretty bad. The thing is I've had so much going on with homework and ball practice and all. I've kind of let it get out of hand, and now I'm so backed up I don't have time to sort it all out. I don't even know where I'd start."

Mom: "Yes, it does look pretty daunting. I think I may be able to help you get started. Grab that pad and pen off your desk, and let's make a list of what all needs to be done."

Marley: "Do I write them in order or what?"

Mom: "Let's just get them down on paper first and worry about the order later."

Marley: "Okay, I need to pick up all these clothes and sort them. I need to take the dirty clothes to the laundry room and put away my clean clothes. I need to take the kitchen stuff back to the kitchen and get rid of all the trash. Whew, that's a lot right there."

Mom: "Keep going. You're off to a fine start."

Marley: "Uh, I guess I need to clean off my bookshelves and straighten up my desk so I can find my school stuff when I need it. I probably need to run the vacuum cleaner. And make my bed."

Mom: "How long has it been since you changed your sheets?"

Marley: "Uh-oh. Busted. Okay, I'll change my sheets."

Mom: "How about the cleanliness quotient? See anything that needs to be cleaned?

Marley: "Well, I guess I need to dust and maybe clean my mirror and stuff."

Mom: "Sounds like you're getting a pretty comprehensive list."

Marley: "Yeah, but Mom, there aren't enough hours left today to get all that done."

Mom: "I'd say that's a pretty accurate assessment of the situation, so what's the solution?"

Marley: "Could I do some things now and some things later this week when I can get to them?"

Mom: "Why don't you look at your calendar and come up with a time completion plan for each of the items you wrote down?"

Marley: "Okay, let's see . . . tonight, I can gather all the food and dirty dishes and get those to the kitchen. I can get all the dirty laundry to the utility room. And I could clean my mirror. Then tomorrow after school I can . . ." (and so it goes until she finishes her list).

Mom looks over the list and helps Marley come up with a feasible timeline to complete all the tasks necessary for her to get her living quarters in order. Mom leaves Marley to start her work. She checks back periodically to give her encouragement and appropriate feedback. She continues to monitor Marley's progress until the job is completed. She then asks her daughter what she learned from the experience. She helps her daughter understand that even the most onerous tasks can be accomplished if they are broken down into reasonable, achievable increments. The goal is to help Marley internalize the concept of taking personal responsibility for her environment as well as her obligation to be a contributing member of the household. Mom wants to help her daughter learn the pride of accomplishing something she previously had not been able to do, but she realizes learners sometimes need support when they begin to try something new. Eventually, Mom will be able to fade out of the process as her daughter realizes her self-efficacy in this setting.

> *What the vast majority of American children need is to stop being pampered, stop being indulged, stop being chauffeured, stop being catered to. In the final analysis, it is not what you do for your child, but what you have taught them to do for themselves that will make them successful human beings.*
>
> —Ann Landers, columnist

Helping Older Children Cope With Failure

Adolescents frequently seem particularly vulnerable to feelings of inadequacy, whether justified or not. Failure can hit them hard, especially if they were generally successful in earlier school experiences. We need to remind them that failure is a natural consequence of trying something new. Failure is not a permanent state of being, but rather it is a necessary step toward excellence. To help them build and maintain growth mindsets, we need to model for them how to recover from failure and move toward the next step. I think we need to teach children how to *fail better.*

MODELING HOW TO FAIL BETTER

Negative Modeling: *"Don't be upset by that grade you received on your report. It wasn't your fault. You are plenty smart, so you'll do better on the next assignment. Don't sweat it."*

Positive Modeling: *"You seem upset by the grade you received on your report. Let's take a look at where you lost points and make a plan for improving your next attempt. I know it's disappointing to get a low grade, but you can learn from this how to improve your future work, and in the long run, that's going to be extremely helpful.*

Negative Modeling: *"You came in next to last? Well, you're way over your head in that field! Let's see if we can find you something you are better at doing."*

Positive Modeling: *"So you were among the last today? Why do you think that happened? Since this is something really important to you, I guess we'd better figure out some ways to help you improve.*

Let's start with some specific skill practice. You do them, and I'll give you feedback."

Negative Modeling: *"You made a failing grade on this test. Maybe it was just too hard for you. I'll see if your teacher will give you some-thing easier to do so you won't have to feel discouraged. I don't want you to feel bad."*

Positive Modeling: *"You made a failing grade on this test. Let's see if we can figure out why. I want you to look at each incor-rect answer again and record why you think you missed it. Here's your coding key."*

DU–didn't understand the question

MR–misread the question

TF–went too fast/didn't check work

DK–didn't know the answer

PW–put the wrong answer by mistake

LO–left out or skipped the question

OR–other reason(s)

"When you have coded your responses, we'll have a better idea of what the problem is, and I'll work with you on finding a solution to doing better on the next one."

When dealing with older kids, the best advice I can give is to actively listen. It is imperative to their healthy development that they learn to manage the freedoms they so desperately want and need. As previously discussed, adults can give students choices without compromising high standards. Students, particularly in middle school, are driven by strong needs for power and freedom. Many times, kids this age become non-communicative with parents and teachers because they sense the people who say they want to have "power with" them are, in fact, trying to exert "power over" them. Kids can sense duplicity in a second, and often, they withdraw or act out when they feel they are being manipulated. It is a delicate matter to balance their need for autonomy with our need to ensure their safety, health, and long-term well-being. The following conversation illustrates an adult who is supposed to be supporting a student but is actually trying to control the student to meet his needs.

Example of an Adult Trying to Have Power Over a Student

Science Fair Day

Lakisha: "Hey, Mr. B! I got my science fair project finished!"

Mr. B: "Well, let me take a look at it."

Lakisha: "Okay, I took all my notes from my journals and wrote my conclusion. I found out some cool stuff. I think you're really going to like this."

Mr. B: "Kisha, why didn't use the stick-on letters I recommended for your posters? Your handwriting is not very even, and it's kind of going down the side."

Lakisha: "Yeah, I know, but it says what I want it to say."

Mr. B: "Well, of course, that's important, but don't you want to redo your paragraphs with some stick-on letters or some stenciled ones? I mean, it's up to you, but it looks a little hurried like it is. I wouldn't want you to lose points for neatness. I think I have some letters here we can use, and if we work through lunch we can get it fixed in time for the fair."

Lakisha: "I thought you said as long as we followed the scientific process on the project we could decide how we want to make our display."

Mr. B: "Well, yes, I did say that, but I meant how you wanted to arrange things on your boards. Remember I told you that judges are usually looking for neat, attractive presentations?"

Lakisha: "I know that, but I like it fine the way it is. We didn't have stick-on letters or stencils at my house, so I did it myself. What's wrong with that? Did we do these projects just for the judges?"

Mr. B: "Oh no, of course not. It's just that we're going to have some high-profile people here judging our science fair, and I don't want you to be embarrassed if your board doesn't look as attractive as the other entries."

Lakisha: "I'm not embarrassed. I don't care what they think. And anyway, you're the one who told us it's not what we 'show,' it's what we 'know,' and I know all about fruit flies now, but if you don't want me in your science fair, fine."

Mr. B: "No, no, I didn't mean that. Of course, it's good you learned about fruit flies. And that's awesome, but I'm just trying to help you."

Lakisha: "I don't need your help. I like my project the way it is."

Mr. B: "But it could be so much better if . . ."

And so it goes with not-so-subtle Coercion 101. The student obviously feels she is being manipulated by her teacher because she is. Apparently, he is more concerned with what the judges are going to think about the project than what his student is feeling. He has his own agenda, and he's not even listening to her.

The adult in this case needs to celebrate with his student about the importance of her investigation, her discoveries, and her joy in learning. If he wants to give her feedback, it should include the crucial elements of her work and not just the slanted letters.

Later, if Lakisha tells him, "The judge said I would have won a ribbon if my poster had been neater," the teacher should answer, "Well, the ribbon's not why you did the project, is it? You learned a lot, and that's certainly worth the time you put into it. If you decide you want to compete for a ribbon next time, then you can remember what the judge told you about this year's project. I'm just excited about what you learned in your investigation. Tell me more about . . ." (and the focus goes back to where it should be, on what the student learned about fruit flies and how working on that project empowered her to do more investigations on her own).

• •

Actively listening to students means trying to hear things from their point of view. Empathy can be empowering rather than entitling when adults are focused on the long-term goals of autonomy, competence, and relatedness for the learner.

Inspiring Young Children

• •
Children have never been very good at listening to
their elders, but they have never failed to imitate them.
—James Arthur Baldwin
• •

Many of the educators with whom I work are also parents of young children. In my workshops, they invariably ask me how to model the philosophy, fall down seven times, get up eight to younger children. This chapter is for adults who deal with preschool and primary students. I included the lyrics to a song by Dr. Monte Selby. Monte is a father, an educator, and a talented songwriter/performer who is well known for his work with motivating students through music. He writes songs with, for, and about kids of all ages. In 2004, while dealing with the delicate issue of potty training for one of his young daughters, he and his wife composed the humorous song "Wiped Out." His own mother was horrified by the lyrics and asked that he not include this particular song on his CD (2006), but he did anyway. In fact, it is now a very popular children's book.

Wiped Out

Michelle Selby, Monte Selby 2006
Used with permission.

"Please somebody wipe me," Nellie said so politely
Bent over with her butt in the air
At four years old she preferred pooping all alone
But wipe herself?—oh no—she didn't dare

After two minutes or three she repeated her plea
Her hands were getting cold on the floor
She listened intently, but no one, evidently
Could hear her through that thick wooden door

So she cranked up the volume shouting out that the restroom
Was starting to stink like a skunk
Her face was getting red on her upside down hanging head
And her nose was filling up with that gunk

No mom, no dad, now Nellie, raging mad
Was forced to an evil ambition
She screamed like a banshee, the pitch rising up wickedly
By George, that would get their attention

But no one came about and she was nearly to pass out
She glared with a look that could kill
She spun the paper on the post hoping nothing would be gross
And wiped!—Hey it was no big deal

She arose with great poise when she heard a familiar noise
Her parents rushed in way too late
"No, thanks," she said with flair, her pointed nose stuck in the air
"I don't need your help at all, go away"

And from that day on forever little Nellie never, never
Asked for help—not a whisper, not a shout
And she felt profoundly older, quite proud, a whole lot bolder
And she announced, "This problem's just been WIPED OUT!"

Adults and children alike love this song because it speaks so clearly to an everyday phenomenon experienced by every family, everywhere. The joy and pride the little girl feels when she learns that she can control her hygiene routines is universally acknowledged.

The story depicts a four-year-old girl stuck on the potty waiting for her parents to come clean her. She screams, cajoles, and otherwise "fit throws," as she demands that they come and take care of her need! In the end, she cannot arouse her parents, so she takes matters into her own hands and does the necessary hygiene maneuvers herself. Belatedly, her parents rush to her side to help her, but as the song tells us, she replies, "No, thanks . . . I don't need your help at all, go away!"

Let's examine the scene in the context of Vygotsky's (1980) zone of proximal development (ZPD). If the little girl were two years old instead of four years old, she would probably lack the essential motor control she needed to do the job, no matter how much her parents had prepared her or how much she wanted to. Additionally, until she saw a need for autonomy over the event, she had no reason to want to learn the necessary steps. For her to know what to do, her parents needed to provide scaffolding. They should have already modeled the procedure for her several times. They needed to provide tissue or other materials the child would need. They needed to explain both the task requirements and the reasons for them. In the song, they had obviously done all that, and the little girl is able to make the final leap from what she had been taught to what she is able to do for herself.

It was a huge achievement for Nellie and a satisfying moment for her parents. Nellie has just taken another step toward autonomy. But let's go a step further. Upon seeing their child beaming with pride, what is the appropriate response from the adults? Some parents might say something like "Wow, you made me so happy! I'm so proud of you! Let's go find you a treat!"

On the surface, those sound like positive, affirming statements that could not do anything but reinforce the desired behavior. But let's look a little deeper into those affirmations. When a child continually hears "You made me so happy" from the adults in their lives, they often learn to think (even unconsciously) that their job is to make the adults in their environment happy. Rather than learning to find a sense of self-efficacy, they learn they have power over making adults happy *or not happy.* That can lead not only to erroneous thinking about their part in the ultimate satisfaction of the adults in their lives, it can also steer them toward some very manipulative behavior (e.g., "I'm mad at you so I won't make you happy now. Look at the mess I just made.").

I have no problem with the words "I'm proud of you," but there are theorists who do. Alfie Kohn (1993), for one, believes that particular phrase is patronizing and paternalistic. He argues that to say "I'm so proud of you" is a bit egotistic and self-serving. While I understand what Mr. Kohn is saying in theory, in reality, I struggle with this admonition. As the mother/stepmother of five sons, I will never relinquish my right to say "I'm proud of you." I guess it's just my mommy gene. And I don't think my boys would want me to stop saying it either. I think as long as parents convey an unconditional acceptance of their children as people, and do not tie the words only to particular achievements or awards, saying the words "I'm proud of you" is neither manipulative nor self-serving. It simply says the adult in the child's life is taking note of growth and appreciates the effort that went into it.

Behavioral psychologists tell us that if we reward extrinsically what ought to be rewarding intrinsically, we rob the learner of the joy of the accomplishment. We also set up unrealistic expectations about why people should do the things they do. In their excitement over their daughter's accomplishment, the parents eagerly wanted to give her some tangible reward to commemorate the event. In doing so, though, haven't they just subtly communicated that the reason one learns to take care of one's own needs is to receive some kind of prize?

Would it not be better to say something to Nellie like "Wow, look at you! You must feel great about what you did! You must feel like such a big girl!" Or feedback could come in the form of interest and questions. "Show me the steps you took." "How did you remember how to do everything?" "Is this something you will be able to do on your own from now on?" "When might you need to still ask for help?"

Be Careful About Indirect Communication

It is also a great time to celebrate with Grandma, siblings, and other close family members. Children so often get feedback from what they overhear adults say. They listen constantly.

Adults need to be cautious about not only what they say to their children but also what they say within earshot of them.

It undermines all the positive feedback of the event for Nellie later to hear Mom say on the phone saying, "Gosh we thought she would never learn to go to the bathroom completely by herself. I don't know what's wrong with her; her sister was totally potty-trained way before this! Well, at least she finally got it! Ugh!" Statements like that will completely undo whatever positives were said in front of the child. Seeds of doubt, anger, betrayal, envy, jealously, and distrust are planted at that moment.

How much more effective would it be for Nellie to overhear mom saying to another adult, "Our daughter is really growing up. Do you know what she did all by herself today? I'm telling you, I am just amazed at what she can do when she puts her mind to it. What a little trooper we have!" The messages here are how much the family values courage, persistence, and effort, all of which can be and should be controlled by the child.

How many times have you heard a parent well within earshot of a child say something such as "Oh that boy is just bad. I'm telling you I don't know what I'm going to do with him. He's just bad!" The teacher in me wants to correct the parent when I witness it. I realize that many times the parent is half-heartedly joking. Sometimes, I think he or she is embarrassed by the child's behavior, and statements like this are his or her way of saying to observers they know the child is acting inappropriately at the moment. I often think they are trying to apologize for having a child who does not meet expectations. In any event, it is wrong. Why would any adult make a comment like that to or about a child who can hear it? Regarding Rosenthal's self-fulfilling prophecy discussed in Chapter 4, it is impossible to imagine how we could expect a child, who is constantly reminded how "bad" he is, to act in any other way. Parents of young children need to be ever vigilant about expressing positive expectations for their children both directly and indirectly. At the same time, it is good to begin building a foundation of self-efficacy, autonomy, and growth mindsets in children while they are young. Here are some examples of appropriate and inappropriate feedback for young children.

Examples of Appropriate and Inappropriate Feedback for Young Children

Bad-Case Scenario

The parents are visiting in their neighbor's home. Their three-year-old, Randy, decides he wants to spin an expensive globe on a stand that sits in the foyer. Mom quickly admonishes him. "Don't touch that, Randy; the Thompsons don't want you to play with it." Randy replies, "I'm not going to hurt it; I just want to see it spin." Mom says, "No, I told you, 'No!'" and she turns her attention away from Randy to speak to her neighbors. Meanwhile, Randy sets the globe in motion. The Thompsons notice and smile weakly but are obviously upset that the child is playing with the orb. Mom raises her voice. "Don't do that, Randy. I said 'No!'" Then she shakes her head and says, "I'm sorry, he's just such a typical boy—into everything! He's so bad. He never listens to a word I say." Meanwhile, Randy continues his joyous exploration of the globe, and the Thompsons are wondering how quickly they can end the visit.

Of course, young children are naturally curious and intrinsic explorers. The beautiful inlaid globe is going to attract them every time. However, Randy obviously has been taught that he can argue his way out of a situation. Rather than responding immediately to his parent's request, he ignores the command and proceeds to do what he wants. Then he hears from the parent that this is what he is expected to do, and he infers that it must be okay because it is not being dealt with.

Better Scenario

Randy decides he wants to spin an expensive globe that belongs to the neighbors. Mom picks up the cue that the neighbors do not want it played with. Mom says in a commanding voice, "Randy, that globe is not yours, and the Thompsons don't want you to play with it." Randy ignores his mom and begins to spin it anyway. Mom takes his hand off the globe, looks him in the eyes, and says, "Randy, you must not touch this globe. We can find you something else to play with, but this globe is off-limits." She leads him away from the globe. The Thompsons say, "Thanks for that; we don't even let our own children play with it." Mom says, "Oh, I totally understand. I have to keep on Randy all the time about touching things. He's just such a tactile learner. He puts his hand on everything, and I have to watch him like a hawk. I can't take him anywhere!"

In this scene, Mom does a better job of immediately addressing the transgression. She even does an admirable job of redirecting his interest. However, in her comments to the neighbors, she undermines anything positive Randy may have learned from the incident because she just reinforced the idea in his head that he is a "toucher," who cannot control himself and does not deserve to be taken to any environment that might challenge his self-control.

Best Scenario

Randy decides he wants to spin an expensive globe that belongs to the neighbors. Mom picks up the cue that the neighbors do not want it played with. In a calm, firm voice, Mom says, "Randy, that globe is so inviting. I'd like to spin it, too, but this one is for looking, not for playing. Later, I can show you a globe at home you can play with, but you must not touch this one." Randy pauses and looks to see if Mom really means it. She does. She focuses her whole atten- tion on Randy until she is sure he understands what he is supposed to do. She may even have to take his hand and direct him toward something else of interest, but she does not break eye contact until he has been diverted. The Thompsons comment, "Wow, your boy sure has good manners for a three-year-old." Mom says clearly, "Well, it's something we work on a lot. Randy amazes me some- times with his respect for other people's things. He's really come a long way in these last few months. Sometimes, it's hard for him to follow the rules, but I see so much growth in him. I can take him a lot more places now that I know I can count on him."

In this instance, Mom empathizes with Randy and redirects him in a calm, assertive manner. She then reinforces the lesson by letting him hear her comment that he really made the effort to make the right choice. She lets him know she appreciates his choice, and she indirectly lets him know that one result of showing self-control is getting to do more cool things with his mom.

Probably some of you are wondering, "But what if Randy kept on spinning the globe no matter what his mother did?" This is where the hard part comes in. I truly believe that most of the fit-throwing and out-of-control behavior I witness nearly every time to go to the grocery store or to a Walmart is mostly parent induced. Usually, it is by acts of omission rather than acts of commission, but it can be either or both. Most children display inappropriate behavior because they get away with it. They sense when their parents are in a hurry, tired, stressed out, or preoccupied. They know they have the edge because they've tried it before, and it worked.

A Familiar Scene

Mom is hurriedly trying to get the groceries selected and purchased because she's running late and needs to get home to start dinner. Two-year-old Connie is tired and hungry and bored. She spies the candy aisle and tells her mom she wants some candy. Mom says, "No, Connie, we're going to be eating dinner in a little while, and you don't need any candy." Connie's predictable response is, "But I want it!" Mom remains firm and continues moving the cart. Connie immediately yells that she wants to get down and tries to stand up in the cart. Mom knows that if she takes Connie out of the cart, the toddler will make a beeline for the candy aisle. Mom says, "No, you are not going to get down." Connie now wails, "I want down, I want down, I want down." Her decibel level and pitch are rising at an alarming rate. Other people are starting to stare. Mom tries to ignore the tirade, but Connie has worked up a good old hissy fit! Mom thinks to herself, "I will never be able to finish my shopping with her embarrassing me like this!" So Mom grinds her teeth and says in Connie's ear, "Okay, young lady, I'll buy you one candy treat, but that's it! Don't you dare ask me for another thing. And this is the last time I am going to bring you to the grocery store with me! Stop acting like a little spoiled brat!"

Connie has just been taught a very direct lesson. If she can cause enough of a stir, she can get her way. In the process, she has temporarily lost her mother's approval, but that's okay for now. She has learned that she has power and can control her mother's choices. Oh boy! Even though her mother threatened to leave her at home next time, she doubts that will happen. She's heard that empty threat before. No worries. Now she has candy and is getting ready to make her next demand.

The reason I understand this story so well is that I was an inadvertent player in similar dramas the whole time my boys were young. I would promise myself that I would not give in to their whims, and more often than I would like to admit, I capitulated for one "good" reason or another. Here's what I have learned since that time.

Best-Case Scenario The optimal solution is not an easy one for the parent, but it is a necessary one. When Connie started her whining and demanding, Mom, of course, could try to reason with her. But Connie is two, and her reasoning ability is limited at this age. Mom needs to demonstrate clearly that she says what she means and she means what she says.

If Connie continues to scream and cry, it would be best if Mom could pick up her cell phone and call someone to come and get the toddler. Ideally, Dad or a close friend would be available, and Connie would hear her mother say calmly into the phone, "John, I am at the grocery store with Connie, and unfortunately, she has decided to pitch a fit on Aisle 2. Would you please come and get her so that I can finish my shopping? Thanks. I promise I'll do the same for you sometime." Then Mom looks at Connie and says, "Honey, it looks like you have lost control of yourself. This is not fun for you or for me, but Mommy has to finish her shopping so I can prepare dinner for our family. Dad is coming to pick you up and take you home because you are making it impossible for me to do my job. I'm really sorry you chose to lose control. I like shopping with you, but I can't have you disturbing all the other shoppers in this store."

Connie learns that she will not be rewarded by her bad behavior. However, if your situation is like mine generally was, you're probably thinking, "Yeah, fat chance I'd find somebody who would come on a minute's notice to pick up my child." The alternative is going to sound like a lot of trouble, and it is, but I really believe it's the best thing to do.

Connie's temper tantrum escalates to the point of disturbing other shoppers. Mom calmly explains to her daughter that her behavior is unacceptable and they will have to leave the store. She retraces her steps and returns her selected items back to their original places. As she is reversing the usual shopping process, she quietly tells Connie that this trip is over. She explains that she and Connie are going directly home, and she will either return at a later time (sans Connie) to do her shopping, or they will just have to make do with items that are already in the house. Mom does not yell, scold, or berate her out-of-control daughter. She just matter-of-factly states the obvious—shopping trips are privileges that must be earned. Poor behavior choices mean that Connie will not be included until she demonstrates more appropriate ways of acting. (Another alternative is to ask a friendly employee if she can temporarily park the cart in the store's walk-in refrigerator while Mom makes other arrangements for her out-of-control child.)

Parents who have done this when their children were small tell me that the payoff is well worth the lost time and inconvenience involved, and they assure me that they did not have to do it more than a few times. Some even report that one time did the trick. The point is that small children need boundaries, and logically the adults in their lives are the ones who must set those boundaries.

Even young children need to understand they are part of a larger scheme of things. Their choices and their efforts directly affect other members of the family. Giving them a treat for being good at the grocery store conveys the idea that they are entitled to a reward for not causing a commotion. It is preferable to help a child learn to control her behavior through a discussion of expectations beforehand, role modeling appropriate behavior throughout the event, and debriefing the event afterward. Think how beneficial it would be for a young child to hear Mom later say to Grandma, "Shopping with Connie is such a joy. She's really good company, and she works so hard to make good choices. Yesterday, at the store, we saw a little boy rolling around on the floor begging for a toy. Connie looked at me and said, 'Uh-oh, his mom's going to have to put back all that stuff in her cart!' Now that she understands how to behave, we have so much fun on our little trips around town."

Children of all ages yearn to make important contributions to the family. They need to understand that they can empower themselves through the choices they make and the effort they put into things. Labeling, scolding, wheedling, and/or pleading do nothing to promote a child's sense of self-efficacy.

Helping Kids Who Are Afraid

Sometimes it's hard to know how far to coax or push a child who is hesitant to try something new. I don't recommend throwing a nonswimmer into a deep lake as my father did to me. With my sons, I wanted to give them a reasonable chance to succeed without scaring the wits out of them. However, sometimes the boys seemed to miss some really fun things because they were afraid for some reason. Two events happened recently with my grandchildren that reminded me how important it is to pay attention and really think about helping young children overcome obstacles.

Earlier this year, my eldest son and I took his two daughters, ages four and eight, to a huge indoor water park. I took four-year-old Olivia to the pool for smaller children and encouraged her to go down one of the two the medium slides or the larger slide built into the young children's play area. She balked and said she was too afraid. I let her take her time wading around the pool and would periodically point out the children younger than she who seemed delighted as they slid down the ramps. I kept steering her toward the slide area, but she would shake her head and tell me she was not going. A couple of times she even walked up the steps and sat at the top of one slide or another, but she each time she would change her mind and walk back down the stairs rather than coast down the slide.

Upon each return to the pool, she would seek me out and proclaim, "I am not going down those slides! It's too scary." I responded, "You don't have to. It's strictly up to you. Personally, I would love to go down one of those slides, but they won't let grown people get on them. This is your vacation, so you should do whatever makes you feel comfortable."

She would ask, "But what do *you* want me to do?" And I would respond, "Whatever you think will be fun for you." I could tell she really wanted me to coax her, but whenever I did, she would quickly shake her head and back away.

I spied a very small slide connected to a miniature climbing tower at the other end of the pool and pointed it out to my granddaughter. I suggested she just sit on the end of it and see what it felt like. She agreed to give it a try. She sat there a few moments and then scooted her backside halfway up the slide and let go. She was beaming when she hit the water. I asked her what it felt like, and she told me it was fun! I assured her that it sure looked like she was having a good time and asked if I could take a video of her coming down the slide. She loved that idea, so I took my iPhone and recorded her accomplishment.

We watched the video together, and I asked her how she might want to improve the movie. She said she would like to try coming down from the top of the slide. She mounted the few steps and down she plunged. A little later, she decided to position herself in the middle rather than close to the edge so that she could slip down without touching the sides.

There were a few miscues, some swallowed gulps of pool water, and even an inadvertent sideways careen, but gradually, she gathered her confidence and mastered her technique. After several successful launches, she began describing to me just how she was maneuvering her way from beginning to end.

Later that afternoon, I watched Olivia's face as she studied the medium slide. I could see the wheels turning inside my little adventurer's head, and sure enough, I heard her yell, "Grammie, watch this!" She resolutely stomped up the steps to the medium slide and this time slid down without any hesitation. She was so proud of herself when she got to the bottom! Of course, the rest of the afternoon was spent repeating her newly learned skills over and over and coming over to debrief me on her learning curve. And I'm sure you've guessed the rest—before we left that day, my little "dare devil" was zipping down the large slide grinning from ear to ear. I'll never forget the sound of that little satisfied voice yelling, "Grammie, I did it! I *did* it! Did you see that?" TUH-Tuh-Tuh-DAH!

The Zip Line Expedition

Shortly after the trip to the waterpark, my husband and I took three of our other sons, their wives, and our two grandsons on a family vacation. It was great fun for my two grandsons to be with their uncles and aunts because we live in five different states and seldom all get together at the same time. We swam, played games, and generally enjoyed being together. Some of us planned an expedition to do a zip line course, and my seven-year-old grandson, Gunner, asked if he could go. I called the company who owned the zip line, and they said as long as he was more than four feet tall and was with adults he could. His mother told him it was an expensive venture that had to be paid for in advance, so if he decided to go, he had better not back out. He chose to go, and I got tickets for everyone who wanted to make the outing. Gunner's mother stayed behind at the pool with his younger brother and a couple of other family members.

One of Gunner's aunts and I decided to stay on the ground and take pictures of the zip liners. We watched as the three brothers, one wife, and my grandson were rigged in their gear. The zip line pros were professional, careful, and thorough. All those who were going down the wires had to sit for a training session. I watched my grandson's eyes grow large as the pros told them what to expect, what to watch out for, and some definite dos and don'ts. There was a small zip line in front of the training area for the adventurers to try out before they committed to the entire two-hour trek. One by one, our family members zipped in front of us and then stood on the platform where their real trip would begin.

After the trial run, I looked at my grandson standing on the platform. His face was pale, and his legs were shaking. His eyes darted around for help as his dad and uncles laughed and told him he was going to be fine. His aunt, who was sitting with me, called to him, "Gunner, if you're scared, you can just sit here with Grammie and me. We'll make sure you have lots of fun. It's fine if you don't want to go."

Immediately, my grandson looked at me. I said, "Nope, that's not true, Gunner. I paid for this, and you're going. Your aunt and I are not going to have any fun while you're gone, so you might as well go along with the rest of your crew. They're counting on you. Your dad, uncles, and aunt will watch out for you. So go."

As soon as they were out of earshot, my daughter-in-law turned to me with an incredulous look on her face. "I can't believe you just said that to him. That is so unlike you to be so heartless."

I smiled and told her, "I wasn't being heartless at all. I was doing what I truly believe is best for him. If we had let him back out at this point, he would have been embarrassed in front of his dad and his uncles. No matter what we said to him afterward, he would know that he backed out in front of three of the people he most admires. There's no way he would recover from that on this trip. It would have ruined his memory of our time together. I trust the pros running this thing, and I know his dad will not let him do anything foolish. Just watch and see what he's like when he gets back."

Periodically, the pros would come in from their various stations after the zip liners had moved on. I asked them how the little guy was doing. They all reported that he was doing great. Apparently, he got braver with every zip and was even asking to lead the line. When they returned from their expedition, my grandson was glowing. He had the biggest grin on his face as he began to recount each phase of the zip lines. Needless to say, it was the highlight of his trip. He is still talking about it. *To reach, to stretch, and to conquer that which one has not done before is one of the most incredible feelings in the entire world. We need to know when to push just a little.* TUH-Tuh-Tuh-DAH!

A Side Note to the Zip Line Story

Ah, be careful of the savvy child. At the end of the adventure, as we walked back to the van, I put my arm around Gunner and said, "How does it feel to face your fears and come out on top? Feels pretty good, huh? I'll bet you are so proud of yourself for taking that risk."

His uncle, my youngest son, Kit, overheard this. He put his arm around me and said, "Mom, how does it feel to put words in your grandson's mouth, so he can tell you exactly what you want to hear and you can put it in your new book?" Oh, the ingratitude of our offspring! Okay, so I'm still learning. . . .

10

FAQs About Teaching Students to Be Successful

- -

Quality is never an accident; it is the result of high intention, sincere effort, intelligent direction and skillful execution; it represents the wise choice of many alternatives.

—attributed to Willa Foster

- -

In my forward, I listed some questions I am typically asked in workshops about student motivation. I am not a trained psychologist nor am I brain researcher. However, I am a teacher with 41 years' experience in education and a mom with 38 years' experience. I have studied student motivation for many years, so with those disclaimers made, I will give you the best advice I have *for now.*

"Seriously, our child really is extremely bright. We all tell her how smart she is all the time because we want her to live up to her full potential. How can that be the wrong thing to do?"

I would recommend you read Dr. Carol Dweck's (2006) book *Mindset* and Chapter 5 of this book. Dr. Dweck worked with gifted and talented children for years as part of her training as a psychologist, and as a child, she was labeled "gifted" herself. She tells the story of one of her elementary teachers who seated the children by their IQ scores and treated them accordingly. Even though Dweck was initially elated to be sitting in the first chair, she came to live in fear that she would somehow be "found out" that she wasn't as smart as the teacher had previously thought. She became obsessed with retaining her status but not with the joy of learning.

A compilation of recent research studies points out it is counterproductive to praise a child for innate talents or gifts. Your daughter cannot control what gifts she got at birth, but she can control what she does with them. Certainly, you want to be supportive of her trying new things, pushing her limits, and putting her heart and her soul into her endeavors. Conversely, if you praise her for being smart, then what happens when she makes a mistake? Is she no longer praiseworthy? She will probably feel that way.

I know it is difficult to refrain from making remarks like "You're so smart" or "You really make us proud with your good grades." But you and those in your extended family need to avoid those kinds of statements. Comments like that will encourage her to make sure she looks smart but not necessarily that she will love to learn. In fact, research shows that generally the opposite is true. Children praised for their grades or high scores become fixated on keeping them rather than on learning for learning's sake. If a teacher or an adult says to you in front of your daughter, "Oh, you're so lucky to have such an exceptionally bright child." A good response would be, "Yes, our little girl was lucky to be born with a great brain, but what we're most proud of us how she keeps trying to grow her brain bigger. She is a wonderfully curious little explorer and a very hard worker."

If you truly want your daughter to live up to her full potential you will praise her for things over which she has influence—how hard she works, how quickly she bounces back from setbacks, how resiliently she deals with failure, and things she should get credit for. Having an innate ability is not a goal nor an accomplishment.

"We told my son that if he will stick with his hockey lessons, we will let him get a new Xbox game. Was that bad?"

I don't like to use the value-laden terms "good" or "bad" when dealing with decisions parents have to make. You are the one who has to decide what is good and what is bad for your family. I will say that research clearly states that using a reward to get a reluctant learner to do a certain task is counterproductive because it further reinforces the idea that the task is unappealing. Hopefully, the reason he is taking hockey lessons in the first place is because he has shown an interest in that sport. If he's not interested, why bribe him to do it? Bloom (1985) found that parental demands are more effective when they play on the child's intrinsic motivation. "If you don't practice music, we sell the piano." "If you don't bring your toys in from the backyard, we donate them to a charity." And, "If you don't go to your hockey lessons, we take you off the team." Just a few of these dramatic lessons will get child's attention and let him know he is responsible for his efforts and his choices.

"In our district there is a big emphasis on differentiated instruction. I like what you are saying about the zone of proximal development, attribution theory, and mindsets. My goal is to give all my students an equal education. So which way is best?"

Thanks to the contributions of Carol Ann Tomlinson (2001) and a myriad of educators, the idea that *everyone deserves an equal education* has been rethought. Proponents of differentiated instruction have debunked the "one size fits all" mentality that was the norm for most schools since they were initially fashioned with factory-like similarity. Basically, what most educational reformists are calling for now is that every student be guaranteed at least a *reasonable* chance at success. I am not sure we can reach consensus on what it "fair" or what is "equitable" in today's challenging world of educational diversity, but I am almost certain most of us can agree on what is "reasonable." When a learner is asked to stretch toward a goal that is just beyond his reach, and that learner is provided with appropriate support, materials, and access, *that* is reasonable. Differentiated instruction provides the tools and strategies for the ideas proposed in this book. They go hand in hand. I am a huge proponent of differentiated instruction; it gives us more ideas and approaches for inspiring students to be self-motivated.

"Are you telling us that basically anyone can be anything they want if they just try hard enough? Is that what I tell my son?"

No, I am not saying that at all. I am saying that anyone can *be better* at what they want if they are willing to put in the time and effort it takes to do so. Certainly, there are physical and mental problems that can act as constraints. Specific physical attributions can put people at a disadvantage for some sports. Of course, we don't want to be too quick to judge on that alone. Doug Flutie, star NFL quarterback, was told he was too short to play professional football. Tom Dempsey, born without toes on his right foot, kicked the longest field goal in NFL history. Ludwig Von Beethoven overcame deafness and depression to become one of the world's greatest composers. Bethanie Hamilton lost her left arm in a shark attack and still became a national champion surfer. And Jessica Cox, born without arms, flies planes, drives cars, and holds a black belt in Tae Kwon Do. So I am very cautious about setting limits on people.

I do think there is a degree of "hard-wiring" that gives certain people an initial advantage in their chosen pursuits. Some individuals seem to have a certain "knack" or proclivity for the tasks they pursue. They seem to have a natural ability to do what is very hard for the rest of us. However, from studies I have read by Ericsson (Ericsson, Krampe, & Tesch-Romer 1993; Ericsson & Smith, 1991), Bloom (1985), and others who study expertise, I have come to believe that whatever benefits there are from being physically or mentally endowed, success will not survive long term without deliberate practice, commitment to hard work, resilience, and passion.

I think it is important that children realize anyone *can get* better at anything with strategic effort. I love to sing. I have a voice that is loud and enthusiastic. The problem is that I have trouble staying on key, and I have no breath control. I am aware when I am off-key, but I don't know how to fix it. Will I ever be the next Idina Menzel, Lea Michele, or Shania Twain? I don't think so. I don't have their training, their skills, or their voice quality. But could I get to be a whole lot better singer than I am right now? Definitely! I could take voice lessons, practice, and do the things great singers do. Will I end up on a Broadway stage? I don't know yet. What I do believe is that I could be a much better singer than I am now if I focused on that particular goal and did the kind of deliberate practice I would need to do to strengthen my ability.

There is also the issue of opportunity for a lot of us. Pink (2009), Gladwell (2008), Colvin (2008), and Syed (2010) all acknowledge that being in close proximity to experts can certainly give someone a leg up. Money is also an issue. Independently wealthy people have the luxury of focusing on their goals with little regard about to how to pay for food, shelter, and other necessities in the meantime. They can travel to the finest schools and hire the best teachers and coaches. It does seem easier for them. And yet, so many of them do not become successful. So it has to be more than that.

I am saying that we have to stop perpetuating this myth of talent or myth of intelligence in our young people. Yes, people have different aptitudes, skills, and competencies, but except for a minute portion of our population who has severe impairments, we can all get better at things that matter to us.

"We were told that our daughter's IQ is just below normal. We're not sure what that means, and we are worried that she won't be able to keep up in school. How do we keep her from giving up when she's up against such overwhelming odds?"

The issue of IQ continues to confound me. Some people who supposed have a very high IQ have trouble tying their shoes, and others reported to have low IQ create ingenious solutions to everyday problems. I think the more we study the brain the more we are aware that a single IQ (intellectual capacity) score is not a reliable way to measure a person's potential abilities. Daniel Goleman (1995) argues that emotional intelligence quota (EQ) is far more predictive of success than any IQ score.

Very few parents realize that Alfred Binet, the "founder of the IQ test," had a very different goal in mind when he devised his instrument. The French psychologist actually believed that all children could learn but at different rates (Wolfe, 1973). His original work was developed to inform educators how they could better serve the needs of diverse children in France—not to sort, cast, and track students by their supposed intelligence quotas. He opposed the use of a single test score to categorize a learner. Binet believed the quality of a person's mind can be changed.

Benjamin Bloom (1985), world-famous American psychologist and founder of *mastery learning,* says that

> After forty years of intensive research on school learning in the United States as well as abroad, my major conclusion is: What any person in the world can learn, *almost* all persons can learn, *if* provided with the appropriate prior and current conditions of learning. (p. 4)

Eric Jensen (2005) and other brain research experts are fully convinced that the brain can literally grow bigger. Study after study has proved that IQ scores can rise 20 points or more in a relatively short period with proper conditions and focus.

Considering that my husband and I were told that one of our sons would never be able to graduate from high school with anything but an attendance diploma, and he recently completed his second master's degree, I am more than a little skeptical of IQ tests. Countless parents have related to me the same story about how their child was labeled a "slow learner" or some other euphemism for low IQ and then with the help of dedicated adults went on to achieve all kinds of noteworthy accomplishments.

I think it is important for your daughter's future that you ignore the IQ score entirely. Make sure her teachers (and you) set high but reasonable goals. Constantly stretch her abilities, and reflect with her on what she has accomplished. Make sure she has many TUH-Tuh-Tuh-DAH! moments. As with our son, hers may be a different or even a harder path to get to wherever she wants to go, but do not for one minute doubt that it is possible.

"At our school we use a schoolwide rewards system to encourage kids to read. I've never been comfortable with it, but most of the other teachers think it's a great idea. What do the experts say about that?"

They say exactly what you think I'm going to tell you. They don't like it either. When educational psychologist John Nicholls was asked what he thought about Pizza Hut's Book-It! Program (one in which students were rewarded with pizzas for reading a certain number of books) he replied only half-jokingly, "Well, expect a lot of fat kids who don't like to read."

That seems rather harsh, and I trust that Pizza Hut was acting with the best intentions when it created its incentive program, but the research is absolutely clear about the long-term price of rewards (see Chapter 6). When the rewards are removed, the behavior will be severely reduced or extinguished. Recent studies on the Accelerated Reading (AR) Program by Marinak and Gambrell (2008) confirmed that students who participated in the AR program showed marked decrease in interest in reading on their own.

It makes sense. If we reward a student for reading, we are basically saying "Look, we know this task in unpleasant, so we're going to give you a little bribe to make it worth your while." Don't get me wrong. I want children to read almost more than I want anything else for them. And I think schools have purchased programs like AR because they feel the same way. But the teachers I talk to say that there is a marked increase of shorter, "big print" books checked out by students trying to earn prizes. They also worry that children are reading more superficially and just skimming the text enough to be able to pass the basic fact tests they need to get their points for prizes. Several say they have children who cannot answer those same questions a week later.

I would not be so critical of incentive programs if I didn't have something better to offer. There are teachers like teacher/author Steven Layne (2009) and teacher/author Donalyn Miller (aka the Book Whisperer; 2009) who have not only managed to inspire students to read incredible amounts of books without using rewards but have also taught others educators how to do the same. Both experts agree that teachers have to know their children and know the literature. Part of the secret is matching the two. Other things they do are set up informal book circles in the classroom for peers to talk about what they are reading, hold one-on-one book discussions with dormant readers, and invite students to give book reviews on stories they would recommend to classmates. I know Dr. Layne personally, and I have had the pleasure of listening to a presentation by Ms. Miller. Both promote growth mindsets, self-efficacy, and a lifelong love for reading in their students. You can find their books listed in the bibliography, and I highly recommend Donalyn's blog at www.bookwhisperer.com. Perhaps, at some point, you can ask your school's decision makers to evaluate whether the incentive program is promoting your long-term goals for your students.

"I teach high school. I have a student who is convinced that he cannot do the work in my class. He won't even try. He totally withdraws when I try to encourage him. I know he could do it, if he wanted to. Do you think he's just faking incompetence for some reason, or is there a possibility he really doesn't know how capable he is?"

As I have pointed out several times in this book, a child's actual ability or talent has little bearing on his perception of it. Highly gifted children with a fixed mindset can be completely undone by a setback or failure and come to see themselves as incapable. Often, students use avoidance or withdrawal to self-medicate; it is their way of coping with an unsure or potentially hurtful situation. As pointed out in Chapter 4, a common reaction to a challenge a student sees as threatening is to exhibit *learned helplessness*. Some students feel so lost and so powerless over their lives they just give up. They feel that nothing they do makes a difference, so why try?

However, few students want to appear dumb or incapable. They would rather say to themselves, "I could do it if I tried, but I'm not going to try," than to ask, "What if I really try, and I still can't do it?" Researchers call this process *self-handicapping*. Students try to preserve their self-esteem by purposefully subverting their success. They are acting out of fear.

And there is the additional chance that your student is acting out of anger toward those in authority—you, his parents, or someone else. He knows the adults in his life are vested in his being successful, so he becomes unsuccessful to demonstrate they cannot coerce him.

From your description, it sounds as though this young man is more scared than anything else. Realize that students often mask fear with other behaviors such as boastfulness, defiance, frivolousness, belligerence, apathy, disinterest, and withdrawal. A good start would be to have a private, frank discussion with this young man to hear what he has to say about his progress in your class. Reassure him you want him to be successful but let him know that the decision is totally his. Try to assess where he is in his learning (not where he ought to be, not where you wish he were, but where he actually *is*) and challenge him to do work that is just beyond his reach. Give him nonjudgmental feedback on his performance and continue to raise the bar as he progresses from one step to the next.

Don't overdo the praise and encouragement. He hasn't earned it yet, and he knows it. Just quietly communicate your interest and belief in him. Try to talk less and listen more even if it means some uncomfortable (for you) silences. He has probably learned to use silence as part of his avoidance technique. Be happy with small steps. Researchers say it takes one month for every birth year to actually change behavior (i.e., if he is 16 years old, he needs about 16 months to fully modify poor habits). Even though you probably only have him for a few of those months, you can certainly get the process started. See if you can bring the parents in on your concerns. If you think depression is involved, don't hesitate to call in a counselor.

> *Once you learn to quit, it becomes a habit.*
> —Vince Lombardi

"I've told my students that failure is not an option. I won't accept failures in my class. What's wrong with that?"

I think most of the time when adults say, "Failure is not an option," they are referring to an attitude of "I won't take no for an answer" or "I won't give up on you, and I won't let you give up on yourself." Sometimes they mean that the idea of letting someone or something (like an institution or mission) fail is so abominable that we dare not even consider it. I have no problem with the optimism and can-do posture evidenced in that thinking. We all need to teach students that grit and spirit are what make us successful human beings.

Several educational experts agree that giving students a failing grade and letting that be the end of it is virtually a cop-out for the kid. He is off the hook and needn't worry himself about the task requirement again. Differentiated instruction specialist Rick Wormeli (2006) suggests that teachers do away with failing grades and replace them with I's for incompletes. Students are told there will be consequences for late work, but nevertheless, they will be held accountable for it. Privileges and desired extras are withheld until the work is completed. Such policies create additional work for the teacher, of course, but the onus should be on the student. The logic behind this type of policy is that every assignment the teacher gives is important, and no one should be allowed to skip essential work. Students need to master the given skills, and teachers should work with them until they do.

I am assuming when you say, "Failure is not an option in this class," you are telling your students that you are willing to do whatever it takes to help them toward mastery. You are letting them know that giving up is not a choice they have. I applaud that.

My only concern with the "Failure is not an option" slogan is that it subtly implies that failure is bad. Since I spent have a large portion of this book talking about how failure is a natural part of life and is something that needs to be embraced and overcome with pride, I would much prefer a slogan that says "Giving up on yourself is not an option." I know it sounds like a manner of semantics, but hopefully, I have shown in this book how powerful word choices are. I'm not in the business of telling teachers how to run their classes. I want each of us to have the autonomy to do what we think is best for our students in our situations. I just ask that we, as teachers, make informed decisions and reflect on how they fit with our ultimate goal—to help students. It's your call.

And, finally, a question I was asked recently in an e-mail:

"I've read some arguments against all this positive attitude push. Some of my activist friends say it's just another way to blame disadvantaged people for their circumstances. What do you say to that?"

Alfie Kohn (2010), among others, has criticized the initiative of telling kids to work harder as way of justifying the fact we (society) are not effectively alleviating the deplorable conditions for many of our youth. He argues that "Rather than being invited to consider the existence of structural barriers and pronounced disparities in resources and opportunities, we're fed the line that there are no limits to what each of us can accomplish on our own if we just buckle down" (p. 7). Like most of my colleagues, I have taught kids who go through more in a month than some of us will go through in a lifetime. My heart breaks for them, but I fail to see how my focus only on the admitted inequities in our world is going to help them succeed.

I will continue to fight for the underdogs in our society and be a persistent advocate for conditions that give everyone a reasonable chance at success. But I do not think people can be helped long-term by anything short of developing self-efficacy and affecting change for themselves. I do not think anyone needs to apologize for advocating determination and fortitude. I don't think the blame game helps anyone. There's a lot of truth in the old adage "People are not responsible for the cards they're dealt, but they *are* responsible for how they play them."

I have witnessed countless people who had few opportunities or advantages rise like a phoenix from the ashes not because someone felt sorry for them or has given them a free ride, but because they used their inner strength and refused to give up.

The Story of a Phoenix

I could recount here one of the many well-known stories told by motivational speakers and writers about any number of celebrities who overcame extraordinary circumstances to become this or that. But I would much rather talk about a relatively unknown little girl, who lived a life that no one would wish on a child, and yet through her own spirit and grit, she has broken a cycle of neglect, irresponsibility, and entitlement. I know this young lady well. She is my daughter-in-law Stephanie. For this book, I asked her to tell me about her childhood, and this is what she said:

> I'm not sure how many schools I attended altogether, but I went to five different schools my eighth-grade year and never lived anywhere longer than a year until I went to college. Along the way, I lived in at least five shelters, lived on the side of the road in California once, and in numerous campgrounds for weeks at a time. I believe I've lived in nine states.
>
> One time we were traveling [moving] from Nevada to Colorado and took the scenic route through Wyoming. We stayed the night in a hotel in Evanston, Wyoming. My dad woke up the next morning, and when he returned from getting some coffee, he decided that he liked it there, so we lived in that motel room for three months. We had an electric skillet, so we could eat in the room.
>
> I started working when I was eight years old as a bus girl at a little place called Calamity Jane's Bar & Grill. I worked there on the weekends and all school breaks for four years. When I was 10, I had three jobs. In addition to Calamity Jane's, I worked as a cashier at the local market, and I babysat. I loved the attention and the money I made, but because I was making decent money, my parents made me buy my own school clothes.

Let me provide some details she did not tell you. She has never met her real father. Her mother and stepfather, both of whom are substance abusers and people who "prefer not to work," brought her up. Her parents often stole the money she earned from working extra jobs to finance their substance addictions. She managed somehow to graduate from high school and, on her own, moved away, enrolled in college, and worked several jobs to pay for it all. Once, on her birthday, her parents called her asking for money to pay for a party they wanted to have for their friends. She was not invited, of course, and they didn't even remember that it was her birthday.

Prior to graduating from college, she studied abroad with the Royal Shakespeare Company and was third runner-up as best new talent of the year in the 2001 Los Angeles Talent Search. For the past five years, she has worked as an account executive for a small advertising firm, and she was recently asked to become a partner (she declined). She was the 2009 Chair of the Austin Chamber of Commerce Ambassadors, and she is on the membership committee for the chamber. She served on the board of the Metropolitan Breakfast Club and was the president of an Austin chapter of the Business Network International.

She is not a huge star or a tabloid sensation, but to me, she is one of the most awe-inspiring people I know. In her quiet way, she has maintained a sense of self and a sense of purpose that have served her well. She never saw herself as disadvantaged or entitled to something she did not earn. But at a very young age, she decided she wanted more, and she tackled the obstacles she needed to make that happen for herself. She is now married to our son, the one who was told he would never graduate from high school and yet went on to earn two master's degrees. With him, she lives in the first home she has ever had. Their firstborn, Liam, just arrived. What an incredible legacy our new grandson is going to have. I am quite sure Andy and Stephanie will teach him to fall down seven times, and get up eight.

Glossary

Attribution Theory

Fritz Heider first introduced the idea of *attribution theory* in 1958 to describe the reasons people give for their success or lack of success on certain tasks. Bernard Weiner (1979, 1980) later developed the basic principle that a person's perceptions or attributions for success or failure determine the amount of effort he will expend on that activity in the future.

Automaticity

Automaticity is the ability to do things without occupying the mind with the low-level details required, allowing it to become an automatic response pattern or habit. It is usually the result of learning, repetition, and practice.

Autonomy

Autonomy is the universal urge to be in charge of one's own life and act in a manner that is self-governing and self-regulating. The belief that one's choices and efforts make a difference is grounded in the assumption that one has at least partial authority over her environment.

Deferred (or Delayed) Gratification

Deferred gratification and *delayed gratification* denote a person's ability to wait to obtain something that he wants.

This attribute is also called impulse control, will power, and self-control.

Deliberate Practice

Psychology professor Dr. Anders Ericsson (1991, 1993) defines *deliberate practice* as an activity specifically designed to improve performance, often with the teacher's help. The task must be repeated many times. Feedback on results is continuously available, and the practice is highly challenging mentally. Whether the pursuit is intellectual or physical, deliberate practice is highly demanding.

Differentiated Instruction

Differentiated instruction is a process made famous by Dr. Carol Ann Tomlinson (2001) that addresses an active, student-centered, meaning-making approach to teaching and learning for students of differing abilities in the same class. The intent of differentiating instruction is to provide students with various avenues to acquire content, to process meaning, and to construct ways to demonstrate their understanding of essential ideas.

Earned Success

Earned success is a gain acquired through service, labor, or work. It is the result of effort or action and is usually associated with purposeful effort.

Emotional Intelligence

Emotional intelligence as defined by Daniel Goleman (1995) is the ability to identify, assess, and manage one's emotions.

Empowerment

As a general definition *empowerment* is a multidimensional social process that helps people gain control over their lives.

It fosters in people additional authority and the capacity to expand power over their environments.

Entitlement

The term *entitlement* refers to the idea that people are endowed with the right to have certain benefits and material goods whether or not they are earned. It is used in this book to describe situations whereby individuals feel they are owed a certain amount of happiness, ease, and/or success as a birthright.

Extrinsic Rewards

Extrinsic rewards can be defined as rewards that come from an outside source, such as the teacher or parent. Rewards include the obvious bonuses, such as prizes, certificates, special privileges, gold stars, stickers, candy gum, redeemable tokens, grades, or even money. Some authorities consider adult praise to be an extrinsic reward as well as more subtle signs of approval such as thumbs up signs, smiles, nods, hugs, or pats on the back.

Fixed Mindset (Entity Theory)

Fixed mindset (entity theory) was developed by Dr. Carol Dweck (2000, 2006) and is based on the idea that some people believe there is a predetermined amount of gifts, talent, skills, intelligence, and the like in each human being. People who have this belief system think that ability and talent are finite entities and are *fixed* from birth.

Flow State

Mihalyi Csikszentmihalyi (1991, 1997) coined the term *flow* to refer to a state of highly concentrated action and awareness, whereby self-consciousness fades away, and there is a solidarity of energized focus on the task. Athletes often call this state "being in the zone." It represents the epitome of intrinsic motivation because the immediate reward for the task is the joy of performing the act itself.

Growth Mindset (Incremental Theory)

Growth mindset (incremental theory) was developed by Dr. Carol Dweck (2000, 2006) and is based on the idea that some people believe that whatever intelligence and abilities a person has, she can always cultivate more through focused effort. People with a growth mindset believe that virtually everyone can get better at anything through education and purposeful work.

Instant Gratification

The psychological concept of *instant gratification* refers to the idea that one wants what he wants right now without having to wait for it or delay pleasure for any reason.

Intrinsic Rewards

Intrinsic rewards can be defined as rewards that are inherent or the natural consequence of behavior without the use of outside incentives.

Learned Helplessness

Learned helplessness is a concept coined by Martin Seligman (1975) and his colleagues. He discovered that when an animal is repeatedly subjected to an aversive stimulus that it cannot escape, it will eventually stop trying to avoid the stimulus and behave as if it is utterly helpless to change the situation. He extended the idea to explain why some people view the world with a "victim mentality" and, therefore, stop trying to improve their lives.

Learned Optimism

Learned optimism is defined by Martin Seligman (2006). He states that optimists are higher achievers and have better overall health. Pessimists, on the other hand, are more likely to give up in the face of adversity or to suffer from depression. Seligman invites pessimists to learn to be optimists by thinking about their reactions to adversity in a new way. The resulting optimism—one that grew from pessimism—is a learned optimism.

Marshmallow Study

The Marshmallow Study, conducted in the 1972 by Stanford University psychology researcher Michael Mischel (1988, 1989), demonstrated how important self-discipline is to lifelong success. He offered a group of four-year-olds one marshmallow, but he told them that if they could wait for him to return after running an errand, they could have two marshmallows. The errand took about 15 minutes. The theory was that those children who could wait would demonstrate they had the ability to delay gratification and control impulse. A longitudinal study of his test subjects proved that those who were able to delay gratification as four-year-olds went on to lead more productive, self-fulfilling lives.

Mindset

Mindset is defined as a habitual or characteristic mental attitude that determines how one will interpret and respond to situations. It is a collection of ideas that influence behavior.

Performance Rewards

Performance rewards are rewards that are available only when the learner achieves a certain set standard (e.g., anyone who has at least 93% correct responses on the homework paper gets a sticker).

Scaffolding

Scaffolding is the act of providing incremental stepping-stones to help learners move forward. Similar to erecting temporary platforms to facilitate movement higher and higher up a building, scaffolding in educational terms means figuratively to use helpful interventions to assist students in moving forward.

Self-Determination Theory

Self-determination theory (SDT) was developed by Edward Deci and Richard Ryan (1995). Conditions supporting the individual's experience of autonomy, competence, and relatedness are argued to foster the most volitional and high-quality forms of motivation and engagement for activities, including enhanced performance, persistence, and creativity. In addition, SDT proposes that the degree to which any of these three psychological needs is unsupported or thwarted within a social context will have a robust detrimental impact on wellness in that setting.

Self-Efficacy

In 1977, Albert Bandura introduced a psychological construct he calls *self-efficacy*. He concludes that the foundation for human motivation is not just about believing one has certain qualities, but rather that one believes she has power over her life. Self-efficacy beliefs provide the basis for human motivation because unless people believe they can affect changes in their circumstances and their lives, they have little incentive to act or to persevere through difficult situations. Self-efficacy is unlike other qualities such as self-esteem because self-efficacy can differ greatly from one task or domain to another.

Self-Esteem Movement

The *self-esteem movement* began in 1969, when psychologist Nathaniel Branden published a highly acclaimed book titled *The Psychology of Self-Esteem*. He argued that "feelings of self-esteem were the key to success in life," and his idea soon became a major trend in education. For nearly four decades, many school programs were built around the concept that helping students feel good no matter what their efforts or accomplishments would lead them to greater happiness and productivity.

Self-Fulfilling Prophecy (Pygmalion Effect)

A *self-fulfilling prophecy* is a prediction that directly or indirectly causes itself to become true, by the very terms of the prophecy itself, due to positive feedback between belief and behavior. Although examples of such prophecies can be found in literature as far back as ancient Greece and ancient India, it is 20th-century sociologist Robert K. Merton who is credited with coining the expression "self-fulfilling prophecy" and formalizing its structure and consequences. Later, Rosenthal and Jacobson (1968) researched the concept by telling teachers that certain children were gifted even though they were not. The students whom teachers perceived to be smarter actually performed better on tests.

Self-Handicapping

Self-handicapping is a term used to describe an action or choice, which prevents a person from being responsible for failure (e.g., "I may not do well on that test today because I don't feel good."). It refers to the strategy of making choices or acting in ways that make it possible to externalize failure and to internalize success. People want to be able to accept credit for any success but have an excuse for any failure.

Self-Motivation

Self-motivation is an individual's embracing of commitment to a task coupled with the personal desire to perform well and to continuously learn. It is exemplified by steadfastness and a desire to always gain knowledge and new skills.

Self-Regulation

Researchers often use the term *self-regulation* when discussing one's ability to postpone actions triggered by the body's basic needs of hunger, fear, thirst, distress, and the like. Many call this ability self-control. As individuals mature, we are better able to tolerate the distress that accompanies an unmet biological or psychological need by postponing or redirecting an inappropriate response (e.g., babies begin to wail the moment they feel hunger, but older children generally are able to wait for the appropriate time to eat rather than howl or grab the first available food).

Success Rewards

Success rewards are rewards given for good performance and might reflect either success or progress toward a goal (e.g., anyone who has at least 93% correct responses on the homework paper or improves his last score by at least 10% receives a sticker).

Task Contingent Rewards

Task contingent rewards are rewards that are available to students for merely participating in an activity without regard to any standard of performance (e.g., anyone who simply turns in a homework paper gets an A).

Vicarious Self-Efficacy

Bandura (1986) first defined *vicarious self-efficacy* as a process of comparison between oneself and someone else's accomplishment (e.g., "If he can do it, so can I.") In this construct, people see someone succeeding at something, and their self-efficacy increases; and where they see people failing, their self-efficacy decreases. This process is more effectual when a person sees himself as similar to his own model. If a peer who is perceived as having similar ability succeeds, this will usually increase an observer's self-efficacy. Bandura postulates that although it is not as influential as experience, modeling is a powerful influence when a person is particularly unsure of himself.

Wait Time

Studies beginning in the early 1970s show that if teachers pause between three and seven seconds after asking higher-level questions, students respond with more thoughtful answers. This finding is consistent at the elementary, middle school, and high school levels.

Zone of Proximal Development

Vygotsky (1980) calls the area between a learner's current unassisted performance level and the point too far for a learner to reach at present (even with assistance) her *zone of proximal development*. In his research, he found that optimal motivation came for study subjects when they were asked to reach just beyond their present state. Zone of proximal development is the region where students are required to stretch to further, but reasonably attainable levels of success.

Discussion Guide

Chapter 1—Self-Motivation

1. Do you believe students today are less motivated than students in the past? Explain why or why not.

2. Occasionally a student will appear to work much harder for Teacher A than for Teacher B. What are some reasons the student might be more self-motivated for Teacher A than for Teacher B?

3. Describe an example in your life when you attempted to bolster another person's self-esteem, and it failed to work. Why do you think you were unsuccessful? Looking back is there anything you would do differently? Why or why not?

4. Describe in detail one of your TUH-Tuh-Tuh-DAH! moments. Talk about what you did, how you did it, and how you felt as you were moving toward your goal. What kept you moving forward? How did you feel when you achieved what you had set out to do?

5. List several entitlement statements you have made or have heard others make. Rephrase them to become empowering statements.

6. What does Bandura mean by *vicarious self-efficacy*? Describe an example of self-efficacy that can be attained in this manner.

7. What kinds of changes need to be made in our schools to do a better job of fostering self-efficacy in young people?

8. List some typical ways adults intentionally or unintentionally undermine children's self-efficacy.

Chapter 2—Zone of Proximal Development

1. In the opening scenario, why doesn't the language arts teacher just tell Elan what a synonym is or ask him to reread the section of his textbook that explains it? What is beneficial about the way she responds to his confusion?

2. The author states, "Nothing is as motivating as hard-earned success." Do you agree with that statement? Why or why not? Cite examples to justify your position.

3. What are the risks of allowing students to work solely in their levels of competence without challenging them to attempt more difficult tasks or concepts?

4. The author states, *"It is not reasonable to hold a student accountable for information presented solely in narrative he cannot read."* Do you agree with that statement? Why or why not? List strategies that could be used with a struggling learner other than just admonishing him to reread the text.

5. There are educators who argue that the ability to read is the cornerstone for every other subject taught in school, so students who cannot read the required text or the assessment instruments should not be able to move forward until they can. Others believe that teachers should offer content knowledge in a myriad of methods so that students progress in their various subject areas while they are honing their reading skills. Where do you stand on this issue? Defend your answer.

6. Describe a scenario in which you were asked to perform a task far beyond your current ability level and no scaffolding was provided. How did you respond to the challenge? What happened to your self-efficacy during the process?

7. Describe an incident in which you had a competent adult providing appropriate scaffolding as you learned a new

skill. How did you respond to the challenge? What happened to your self-efficacy during the process?

8. What are some general strategies for assessing the ZPD in learners?

Chapter 3—Self-Regulation and Deliberate Practice and Failure

1. Do the findings from Mischel's (1988) classic marshmallow study confirm or challenge your beliefs about students and *instant gratification?* Explain your answer.

2. Discuss various methods you have used (or have observed someone else use) to help students learn to control impulsivity. What are additional strategies you are willing to try?

3. Do you think self-control can be and/or should be taught? Elaborate on your response.

4. The author offers an explanation for why she thinks the words *for now* are important when helping students learn self-regulation. What are some other words or strategies adults can use to assist students learn to delay gratification?

5. Give an example of *deliberate practice* and explain how it would vary from what most people would call a practice session. How would you guide a student toward *deliberate practice?*

6. Anders Ericsson (1991) states that it takes 10,000 hours of practice for someone to become an expert at anything. Do you think students today believe that? Explain your answer. Why is it important for adults to convey to students that true expertise usually takes a very long time?

7. In a classroom of students who are at different mastery levels in a certain area, how do you ensure that each one is working within his or her ZPD?

8. How can adults better help students deal with issues of failure? Give examples.

Chapter 4 — Attribution Theory

1. Describe how praise can sometimes do more harm than good. Give examples from your experience.

2. How can helping students understand the concept of attribution theory help them gain self-efficacy? Give examples of how adults can do this.

3. Discuss students you presently teach or you have previously taught who show indications of *learned helplessness*. How have you previously dealt with the problem? Is there anything you would do differently now?

4. Observe an adult giving feedback to a child. You can visit a classroom, listen to a casual conversation, view a movie or TV program, or record yourself interacting with a student. Review the feedback that was given and discuss its value toward student growth.

5. In small groups, practice giving effective feedback. Assign one member to act as the student and one member to act as the teacher. Role-play the following scenarios or make up your own. Have the remainder of the group make notes and give other suggestions for helpful feedback. Rotate the job assignments each time.

Possible Scenarios

a. Joey is frustrated about the test he is taking. He tries to hand it in incomplete and early. He tells you it is the best he can do because he has never been good at this subject.

b. DeMarcus turned in an essay that was imaginative and interesting, but there are loads of grammatical errors, and his handwriting is so bad you can barely read the story.

c. Abigail tried out for the lead in the senior play, but she didn't get it. She is angry that her nemesis "conned her way" into getting the part.

    d. Rick earned a C on the project he turned in. He tells you that a C is plenty good enough for him.

    e. Rosa complains that she studied "really hard" for the test, but you asked the wrong questions.

    f. Sheila just made the first A she has ever made on one of your quizzes. She and her classmates believe that she was extremely lucky to have made the highest grade in the class.

    g. Henry tells you he knows the content, but when you time him his brain "freezes up," and he's not able to remember what he knew right before he came into class.

    h. Zoe's science fair project is far superior to anything you have seen before from a student her age. It is an achievement you never expected from her or any other student you've taught. Her father is a science researcher.

6. Do adult expectations influence student behavior? Explain your answer and give examples.

7. What kinds of circumstances undermine the positive effects of self-fulfilling prophecy? Does the belief that one is loveable and capable overcome all adversity? Justify your response.

8. List several ways teachers communicate both positive and negative expectations in the classroom. Record both verbal and nonverbal cues. Can you describe some that are subtle but still powerful?

Chapter 5—Mindset—The Key to Self-Motivation

1. In "Elizabeth's Dilemma," Dweck (2006) gives five possible choices. Did your initial response change after you read the narrative describing Dweck's explanation about each choice? Why or why not?

2. What is IQ? Do you believe that intelligence is malleable? Do you think people can actually increase their IQs? What evidence do you have to support your belief?

3. Describe a learner you know who has a *fixed mindset*. Discuss the things that stand out to you as evidence that the student falls into this category. Do you think there are long-term advantages to having a *fixed mindset?* What are they?

4. Describe a learner you know who has a *growth mindset*. Discuss the things that stand out to you as evidence that the student falls into this category. Do you think there are long-term advantages to having a *growth mindset?* What are they?

5. List some things you have said to students in the past that reinforce a *fixed mindset*. How would rephrase your comments to reinforce a *growth mindset* instead?

6. Carol Dweck's (1999, 2000, 2006) mindset theory derives from her initial interest in attribution theory. How do you think her research on attribution theory led her to her conclusions about mindsets?

7. Discuss a gifted person (in intelligence, athletic, or artistic ability) you know of whose *fixed mindset* led him or her to less than desirable outcomes in his or her life. Describe how a *growth mindset* could have changed things for that person.

8. What is the difference between working harder and working smarter? How can you guide a learner to work smarter?

Chapter 6—Examining Rewards

1. What is your personal philosophy about the use of rewards to motivate students? Have you always felt that way, or has something changed your mind? Describe how you came to believe what you do about rewards.

2. Recount an incident where you observed the use of rewards backfiring on the adult using them with children. Explain why you think things turned out as they did.

3. Do you think some kinds of rewards are more harmful long-term than others? Discuss which ones, if any, have the most negative effects and tell why you think that is.

4. List some of the most common meaningless affirmations adults make about student work. Next, list some purposeful, intentional statements adults could use to provide more effective feedback. (Try to stay away from "I statements.")

5. Which areas of the subject(s) you teach do students seem to find the least engaging? What are some ways, other than using rewards, you can encourage them to tackle the more mundane tasks?

6. What is meant by the term "praise junkie"? What factors lead to this so-called condition? What kinds of praise tend to foster negative consequences either short term or long term?

7. Do you believe there are any constructive long-term benefits of rewards? Explain if and when you think they are appropriate or why you think they are never appropriate.

8. Some districts and schools are moving to mandated systemwide rewards to boost student test scores and help close the achievement gap. Do you support that idea? Why or why not?

9. What do you do if some of your students' parents have a view about rewards that is diametrically opposed to the system you use in your classroom?

Chapter 7—Autonomy, Time, and Flow

1. Chapter 4 described Miller's (1975) littering experiment in which one of three groups of students were treated with adult persuasion. The long-term effects of the persuasion were not effective. Relate the results to the concept of student autonomy. What implications do the results of this study have

for teachers and parents who are trying to change student behavior?

2. List specific ways you encourage student autonomy in your classroom. Which ones work the best for your students? What are some additional strategies you might try?

3. Create five statements you or another teacher might say to students that are overtly or covertly controlling. Rewrite those examples to make them autonomy supportive without being demotivating.

4. How long do you typically wait for a response when you have asked a student a direct question? (*You may have to have someone time you to get an accurate assessment.*) Have you considered the research on wait time when questioning students? What are the benefits of requiring students to wait three to seven seconds before answering?

5. If a student is struggling with a response to a question, what are some appropriate ways a teacher can help her try to uncover the answer? Why is it important to stay with the student and not just move on quickly to the next class member?

6. When do you think it is suitable to give students timed assessments? Why? Are there instances when you feel it is not appropriate to give timed assessments? Why?

7. Describe a time when you experienced what Csikszentmihalyi (1991, 1997) calls *flow*. How did you get to that state? What did it feel like?

8. If you could design the most advantageous schedule for student learning at your school, what would a typical day be like in your classroom?

Chapter 8—Helping Students Stay Motivated as They Get Older

1. What are some methods you have used in dealing with students who procrastinate? Name something mentioned

in Chapter 8 you have not used before but are willing to try. How do you think this new strategy will be helpful?

2. There are current education experts who believe that late student work should be accepted without a penalty. Does this practice enable students to procrastinate? Should there be a consequence for assignments that are not turned in on time? Discuss and defend your answer.

3. Talk about various ways to help older students learn to *fail better.* Should adults actually be teaching kids about failure when our ultimate goal is to teach them to succeed? Explain why or why not.

4. What is the difference between having *power with* a student as opposed to having *power over* a student? Give examples.

5. Discuss why you think students sometimes feel they are being manipulated by the adults in their lives. When do you think it is appropriate to share power with students?

6. Edward Deci and Richard Ryan (1995, 2000), developers of self-determination theory, believe there is a universal innate need for competence, autonomy, and psychological relatedness. How can teachers help older students develop a sense of psychological relatedness (the universal need to want to interact, to connect to, and to experience caring for others)?

7. Do you think it is harder for students to maintain their sense of motivation as they grow older? Discuss your opinion and give examples to support your beliefs.

Chapter 9—Inspiring Young Children

1. Why is it important for parents to monitor not only what they say directly to children but also what they say in front of young learners?

2. Do you think it is appropriate for parents of young children to say things such as "Good girl!" or "Good boy!" when the child pleases the parent? Why or why not?

3. In the story about Nellie and her mastery over her bathroom hygiene, what would be the appropriate feedback to give her about her accomplishment?

4. Cite examples of instances where you have heard adults say inappropriate comments about children within their earshot. How did you feel about what was said? Why did you feel that way?

5. How can parents and teachers foster a sense of competence (being effective in one's environment) in younger children? Name some specific strategies.

6. Discuss an instance in which you helped a young learner overcome an obstacle. How did you decide when to push and when to pull back as you tried to get the child to try something new? Are there key things to look for when encouraging a child to take a risk? What are they?

7. Name some ways that adults sometimes inadvertently contribute to *learned helplessness* in younger children. What is the difference between being supportive of a student and enabling a student to be helpless? Give examples.

Chapter 10—Additional Questions to Consider

1. What kind of praise do you typically give students who are extremely bright and/or talented? Has this book persuaded you to alter your praise statements? Explain why or why not.

2. Getting kids to do certain tasks by offering them a reward is common practice in most schools and homes. Has this book changed your mind in any way about the use of rewards as incentives? Explain why or why not.

3. Explain how differentiated instruction supports the concepts of self-efficacy and self-determination.

4. America has taken pride in telling its citizens, "People can be anything they want to be through hard work and

determination." After reading this book, would you modify that statement? Justify your response.

5. How do you respond to parents who base their expectations for their children on previous achievement test scores or on an IQ assessment?

6. What do you do if your philosophy about using rewards is in conflict with the way your school or system mandates?

7. Has anything in this book changed your mind or affirmed your beliefs about dealing with reluctant learners? Describe an *aha moment* you had during any of your readings or group discussions.

8. What is your philosophy about the role of failure in the learning process? Did anything in this book study influence your thinking? Do you plan to do anything differently with learners regarding the concept of failing? Explain why or why not.

9. Do you think that the idea of *positive thinking* is disrespectful to the countless students whose circumstances are abominable and beyond their control? Do you agree that an emphasis on *self-efficacy* is just another way to blame disadvantaged people for their circumstances? Explain why you feel the way you do.

10. Describe your own Phoenix Story. Talk about a person you know or know about who overcame incredible obstacles to become a self-actualized, successful individual. Explain how you think that happened. Would it benefit students to hear such stories? Discuss why or why not.

References

Amabile, T. (1996). *Creativity in context*. Boulder, CO: Westview Press.

Ames, C. A. (1990). Motivation: What teachers need to know. *Teachers College Record, 91,* 409–421.

Ariely, D. (2011, April 12). How self-control works. *Scientific American*. Retrieved from http://www.scientificamerican .com/article.cfm?id=how-self-control-works

Bandura, A. (1986). *Social foundations of thought and action: A social cognitive theory*. Englewood Cliffs, NJ: Prentice Hall.

Bandura, A. (1989). Human agency in social cognitive theory. *American Psychologist 44,* 1175–1184.

Bandura, A. (1997). *Self-efficacy: The exercise of control*. New York, NY: Freeman.

Bloom, B. S. (1985). *Developing talent in young people*. New York, NY: Ballantine Books.

Branden, N. (1969). *The psychology of self-esteem*. New York, NY: Bantam.

Brophy, J. E. (1981). Teacher praise: A functional analysis. *Review of Educational Research, 5,* 5–32.

Canter, L. & Canter, M. (1976). *Assertive discipline: positive behavior management for today's classroom*. Bloomington, MN: Solution Tree Press.

Chance, P. (1992). The rewards of learning. *Phi Delta Kappan, 74*(3), 200–207.

Chua, A. (2011, January 8). Why Chinese mothers are superior. *The Wall Street Journal*. Retrieved from http://online.wsj

.com/article/SB100014240527487041115045760597135286 9
8754.html#printMode

Colvin, G. (2008). *Talent is overrated: What really separates world-class performers from everybody else.* London, England: Penguin Group.

Csikszentmihalyi, M. (1991). *Flow: The psychology of optimal experience.* New York, NY: Harper Perennial.

Csikszentmihalyi, M. (1997). *Finding flow: The psychology of engagement with everyday life.* New York, NY: Basic Books.

Deci, E. L., with Flaste, R. (1995). *Why we do what we do: Understanding self-motivation.* London, England: Gross/Putnam Books.

Deci, E. L., & Ryan, R. M. (1995). Human autonomy: The basis for true self-esteem. In M. Kernis (Ed.), *Efficacy, agency and self-esteem* (p. 3149). New York, NY: Pienum.

Dweck, C. S. (1999). Caution—praise can be dangerous. *American Educator, 23*(1), 4–9.

Dweck, C. S. (2000). *Self-theories: Their role in motivation, personality, and development.* Philadelphia, PA: Psychology Press.

Dweck, C. S. (2006). *Mindset: The new psychology of success.* New York, NY: Random House.

Dweck, C. S. (2008). The secret to raising smart kids. *Scientific American Mind 18*(6), 36–43.

Ericsson, K. A., Krampe, R. T., & Tesch-Romer, C. (1993). The role of deliberate practice in the aquistion of expert performance. *Psychological Review, 100*(3), 363–406.

Ericsson, K. A., & Smith, J. (Eds). (1991). *Toward a general theory of expertise: Prospects and limits.* Cambridge, England: Cambridge University Press.

Gladwell, M. (2008). *Outliers: The story of success.* New York, NY: Little, Brown.

Goleman, D. (1995). *Emotional intelligence.* New York, NY: Bantam Books.

Hallowell, E. M. (2004). *A walk in the rain with a brain.* New York, NY: HarperCollins.

Hallowell, E. M. (2007). *Crazy busy: Overstretched, overbooked, and about to snap! Strategies for handling your fast-paced life.* New York, NY: Ballantine Books.

Heider F. (1958). *The psychology of interpersonal relations.* New York, NY: Wiley.

Jensen, E. (2005). *Teaching with the brain in mind* (2nd ed.). Alexandria, VA: Association for Supervision and Curriculum Development.

Knaus, W. (1997). *Do it now: Break the procrastination habit* (Rev. ed.). Somerset, NJ: Wiley.

Knutson, B., Adams, C. M., Fong, G. W., & Hommer, D. (2001). Anticipation of increasing monetary reward selectively recruits nucleus accumbens. *Journal of Neuroscience, 21.* Retrieved from http://www.jneurosci.org/content/21/16/RC159.full.pdf

Kohn, A. (1993). *Punished by rewards: The trouble with gold stars, incentive plans, A's, praise, and other bribes.* Boston, MA: Houghton Mifflin.

Kohn, A. (2001, September). Five reasons to stop saying,"Good job!" *Young Children, 56*(5), 24–28.

Kohn, A. (2010, Fall). Bad signs. *Kappa Delta Pi Record.* Retrieved from http://www.alfiekohn.org/teaching/badsigns.htm

Kriegel, M. (2007). *The pistol: The life of Pete Maravich.* New York, NY: Free Press.

Layne, S. (2009). *Igniting a passion for reading: Successful strategies for building lifetime readers.* Portland, ME: Stenhouse.

Lehrer, J. (2009). Don't! The secret of self-control. *New Yorker.* Retrieved from, http://www.newyorker.com/reporting/2009/05/18/090518fa_fact_lehrer

Lepper, M, Greene, D. & Nibett, R (1973). Undermining children's interest in extrinsic reward: A test of "overjustification" hypothesis. *Journal of Personality and Social Psychology, 28,* 129–137.

Levine, M. (1990). *Keeping a head in school: A student's book about learning abilities and learning disorders.* Cambridge, MA: Educators.

Levine, M. (1992). *All kinds of minds: A young student's book about learning abilities and learning disorder.* Cambridge, MA: Educators.

Marinak, B. A., & Gambrell, L. B. (2008). Intrinsic motivation and rewards: What sustains young children's engagement with text? *Literacy Research and Instruction, 47,* 9–26.

Marzano, R. J., Pickering, D. J., & Pollock, J. E. (2001). *Classroom instruction that works: Research-based strategies for increasing student achievement.* Alexandria, VA: Association for Supervision and Curriculum Development.

Merton, R. K. (1948/1968). The self-fulfilling prophecy. *Social theory and social structures* (2nd. ed., pp. 475–490). New York, NY: Free Press.

Miller, D. (2009). *The book whisperer: Awakening the inner reader in every child.* Somerset, NJ: Jossey-Bass.

Miller, R. L, Brickman, P., & Bolen, D. (1975). Attribution vs. persuasion as a means of modifying behavior. *Journal of Personality and Social Psychology. 31,* 430–441.

Mischel, W., Shoda, Y., & Peak, P., (1988). The nature of adolescent competencies predicted by preschool delay of gratification. *Journal of Personality and Social Psychological Association, 54*(4), 687–696.

Mischel, W., Shoda, Y., & Rodriguez, M. L. (1989). Delay of gratification in children. *Science, 244,* 933–938.

Mueller, C. M., & Dweck, C. S. (1996, April). *Implicit theories of intelligence: Relation of parental beliefs to children's expectations.* Poster session presented at Head Start's Third National Research Conference, Washington, DC.

Nike (creator). EricFalcon1 (Poster). (2008a, November). Failure: Michael Jordan commercial [video] Retrieved from www.youtube.com/watch?y=m-EMOb3ATJ0

Nike (creator). Diegoris23 (Poster). (2008b, April 19). Maybe: Michael Jordan Commercial [video] Retrieved from www .youtube.com/watch?v=woOu_4l3lio

Noddings, N. (1992). *The challenge to care in schools.* New York, NY: Teachers College Press.

Piaget, J. (1974). *To understand is to invent.* New York, NY: Grossman.

Pink, D. (2009). *Drive: The surprising truth about what motivates us.* New York, NY: Penguin Group.

Reyes, C. (2011a). *When children fail in school: Understanding learned helplessness.* Retrieved from http://educationforth e21stcentury.org/2011/02/when-children-fail-in-school -understanding-learned-helplessness/

Reyes, C. (2011b). *When children fail in school part two: Teaching strategies for learned helplessness students.* Retrieved from http://www.edarticle.com/article.php?id=1842

Rosenthal, R. (1994). Interpersonal expectancy effects: A 30-year perspective. *Current Directions in Psychological Science, 3,* 176–179.

Rosenthal, R., & Fode, K. (1963). The effect of experimenter bias on the performance of the albino rat. *Behavioral Science, 8,* 183–189.

Rosenthal, R., & Jacobson, L. (1968). *Pygmalion in the classroom: Teacher expectations and pupils' intellectual development.* New York, NY: Holt, Rinehart and Winston.

Rosenthal, R., & Jacobson, L. (1992). Expanded edition. *Pygmalion in the classroom: Teacher expectation and pupils' intellectual development.* New York, NY: Irvington.

Rowe, M. B. (1987). Wait time: Slowing down may be a way of speeding up. *American Educator, 11,* 38–43, 47.

Russell, B. (2009). *How "entitlement attitudes" harm America.* Retrieved from http://www.wnd.com/index.php?fa =PAGE.view&pageId=92966#ixzz1YVULg3l6

Ryan, R., & Deci, E. (2000a). Intrinsic and extrinsic motivations: Classic definitions and new directions. *Contemporary Educational Psychology 25,* 54–67.

Ryan, R. M., & Deci, E. L. (2000b). Self-determination theory and the facilitation of intrinsic motivation, social development, and well-being. *American Psychologist, 55,* 68–78.

Seligman, M. E. P. (1975). *Helplessness.* San Francisco, CA: Freeman.

Seligman, M. E. P. (2006). *Learned optimism: How to change your mind and your life.* New York, NY: Vintage Books.

Selby, M. (2006). Wiped out. In *The Teacher's Lounge* [CD]. Nashville, TN: MDM.

Syed, M. (2010). *Bounce.* New York, NY: HarperCollins.

Silver, D. (2005). *Drumming to the beat of different marchers: Finding the rhythm for differentiated learning.* Nashville, TN: Incentive.

Spock, B. (1973). *Dr. Spock's baby and child care.* New York, NY: Simon & Schuster.

Sousa, D. A., & Tomlinson, C. A. (2011). *Differentiation and the brain: How neuroscience supports the learner-friendly classroom.* Bloomington, IN: Solution Tree Press.

Tauber, R.T. (1997). *Self-Fulfilling prophecy: A practical guide to its use in education.* Westport, CT: Praeger.

Tomlinson, C.A. (2001). *How to differentiate instruction in mixed-ability classrooms* (2nd ed.). Alexandria, VA: Association for Supervision and Curriculum Development (ASCD).

Tomlinson, C.A. (2010). *A baker's dozen indicators of quality.* Retrieved from http://www.caroltomlinson .com/2010SpringASCD/Tomlinson_QualityDI.pd

Vygotsky, L. S. (1980). *Mind in society: The development of higher psychological processes.* Cambridge, MA: Harvard University Press.

Weiner, B. (1979). A theory of motivation for some classroom experiences. *Journal of Educational Psychology, 71,* 3–25.

Weiner, B. (1980). A cognitive (attribution)-emotion-action model of motivated behavior: An analysis of judgments of help-giving. *Journal of Personality and Social Psychology, 39*(2), 186–200.

Wolfe, T. (1973). *Alfred Binet.* Chicago, IL: University of Chicago Press.

Wormeli, R. (2006). *Fair isn't always equal: Assessing and grading in the differentiated classroom.* Portland, ME: Stenhouse.

Zaslow, J. (2007). The entitlement epidemic: Who's really to blame? *The Wall Street Journal.* Retrieved from http://online.wsj.com/article/SB1184804326435710

Index

CORWIN
A SAGE Company

The Corwin logo—a raven striding across an open book—represents the union of courage and learning. Corwin is committed to improving education for all learners by publishing books and other professional development resources for those serving the field of PreK–12 education. By providing practical, hands-on materials, Corwin continues to carry out the promise of its motto: **"Helping Educators Do Their Work Better."**

AMLE.

The Association for Middle Level Education is dedicated to improving the educational experiences of young adolescents by providing vision, knowledge, and resources to all who serve them in order to develop healthy, productive, and ethical citizens.